The Created Person and the Mystery of God:

The Significance of Religion in Human Life

By

John Janaro

© 2002, 2003 by John Janaro. All rights reserved.

No part of this book may be reproduced, stored in a retrieval system, or transmitted by any means, electronic, mechanical, photocopying, recording, or otherwise, without written permission from the author.

ISBN: 1-4107-0289-8 (e-book)
ISBN: 1-4107-0290-1 (Paperback)

Library of Congress Control Number: 2002096448

This book is printed on acid free paper.

Printed in the United Sates of America
Bloomington, IN

1stBooks – rev. 04/11/03

*The Created Person and the Mystery of God:
The Significance of Religion in Human Life*

Contents:

Preface: vii

Part I: The Created Person And The Mystery Of God: An Essay In The Philosophy Of Religion 1

Part II: Thomistic Roots Of A "Fundamental Theology": Studies In The Thought Of Jacques Maritain 83

Part III: A Complementary Approach: Outline Of The Existential Religious Philosophy Of Luigi Giussani 165

Part IV: Jesus Christ Preached By The Church: Some Suggestions Toward the Solution of the Problem of Man 181

Conclusion 239

Preface:

The studies in this book propose to approach in various ways the central issue about the truth of man's relationship to God. It follows that what we are dealing with is the deepest and most meaningful truth about man himself. This immediately raises issues that are not primarily theoretical and methodological, but existential. It can scarcely be denied that human beings need to know the truth about who they are and what they are made for. We need to know this truth in order to live as we ought to. But how can we know it, not just in the manner of an empirical analysis, not simply as facts and information, but as *wisdom* (i.e. as an perception that orders life)? How can we know the truth that is adequate to us as *persons*? As persons, we desire to know the meaning and value of other persons and things, and not only a set of facts about them analytically schematized into notional systems of information. We desire, moreover, to know the Source of meaning and value, and the ultimate purpose of our lives and of all things. Even in today's culture, in spite of all our selfishness and acquisitiveness, this deep and strange aspiration endures within us and expresses itself in various forms.

Moreover, the human person desires to possess wisdom with a loving intelligence that goes beyond the realm of corruption, the implacable laws of death and decay and the seemingly inescapable violence of human ambition, envy, and partisanship that obscures any discourse about ultimate truth. But how can we know this truth which is of such vital significance to our humanity? Here in particular our society is at a loss and does not know how to guide us.

Here indeed, our friends, our co-workers, our neighbors, perhaps even our relatives, brothers and sisters, or parents are at a loss. What makes things true, good, and beautiful—indeed what is Truth, Wisdom, Goodness, Beauty?

The reflections in this book are merely a preamble to the great dramatic proposal of history: that Jesus of Nazareth is the answer to man's thirst for mystery and his search for meaning. What Jesus has proposed and continues to propose through the "extension" of His presence in history—the Church—is that the length and breadth, the height and depth of wisdom is possible for man. Jesus has brought it; He has given it; indeed it is nothing less than Himself, and man takes hold of truth by allowing himself to be possessed by Him who is The Truth.

In this way man can embrace, with loving conviction, Jesus who is Truth and Beauty and Wisdom and Goodness made flesh—that is to say, *present in history and given to man*. The "Good News" is that—in the great imagery used by so many classical Christian writers—the darkness of reality's mystery is giving way to the dawn; the Source and the Hope of man's existence has spoken to him in history, has revealed the way for man His creature to become everything man was created to be.

Our purpose in these pages is to explore what the mind and heart of man can know about God and about man's own position in front of God. This ultimately will provide for us the ability to see what it is about man—about his life, about his grandeur and his misery—that makes the Good News of Jesus so wonderfully good and liberating for the whole of the human person. The Mystery who gives man his being has drawn close to him, spoken to him, and become his companion within history. What we want to begin to understand is that this gift, this message, this continued presence of God in man's history is an affirmation of the value of man himself; it corresponds to all that is most noble and beautiful in man, and it heals what is broken in him.

God addresses man His creature according to the fullness of the dignity of his humanity—God addresses man *as man*, as a person. Man therefore is not called to adhere to God in a way that contradicts his humanity; he adheres to God with the full richness of his nature and his capacities—that is to say, by a *fully personal act*—an act that fully engages his reason and his freedom; an act that does justice to his reason and emerges from the depths of his freedom; an act of knowledge and love.

With these things in mind, we shall first attempt (in Part I) to propose some of the more basic points of the philosophy of religion. Although Christianity has formed the historical context for the development of the philosophy proposed here, we want to see that its points are founded on human reason and can be understood without direct recourse to historical divine revelation and faith.

In Part II, we will enrich the theoretical foundations of the conclusions of Part I by presenting several studies on the epistemological approach to God and the distinctive metaphysical character of "natural theology" as expounded by the great twentieth century Thomist philosopher Jacques Maritain. As we shall see in Part I, Thomas Aquinas establishes the key philosophical insight that helps us to see how man can arrive at the fully rational conviction of the existence of God. Maritain's natural theology is worthwhile not only as a faithful exposition of the approach of Thomas Aquinas, but also for its own original development of that thought. The studies in Part II serve as an introduction and provocation for further consideration, and do not seek to be a comprehensive exposition of Maritain's thought on the philosophical approach to God.

Part III is a brief introduction to a highly original approach to the religious question as proposed by the Italian theologian Luigi Giussani in his seminal work *The Religious Sense*. This approach, which makes an important contribution to the proposal presented in Part I, is compatible with and complimentary to the classical metaphysics and epistemology of Thomas Aquinas; yet it entails also new insights of a phenomenological order and presents a particularly effective psychological pedagogy for leading the human mind to recognize the existence of the mystery of God.

Finally, Part IV provides a transition from the philosophy of religion to a special consideration of Divine revelation as proposed by the Christian tradition. The particular emphasis here is on how the gospel–while infinitely surpassing anything conceivable by human reason–fulfills in an eminent manner the religious character of human existence, and thereby proves itself to be of the utmost intrinsic importance to man as man.

Part I: The Created Person and the Mystery of God: An Essay in The Philosophy of Religion

I. INTELLIGENCE, FREEDOM, AND PRAYER

Let us begin by outlining the hypothesis we wish to examine in these pages. What we propose is that man's experience of the things of the world as *created*, and of himself as creature, is the great sign that opens him up in the fullness of his humanity to the Mystery of God. This openness is the proper realization of human nature, and constitutes man's vital receptivity to the design and intention of God regarding his existence. In Christianity, we affirm that what has happened, *in fact*, is that God has fashioned an extraordinary destiny for man, and He enables man to accomplish this destiny by communicating to him a participation in Divine life through Jesus Christ.

This means, however, that God's intervention in history brings about something *more* than a mere confirmation and clarification of man's experience of himself. Rather, Divine historical revelation announces that man is called to a purpose that he never could have imagined or conceived within the scope of his own created nature even considered in its openness to God. Nevertheless, this *super*-natural destiny is *in fact* God's design for man's life (and it is a design that–even thought it transcends utterly any possibility contained within man's religious openness–supereminently fulfills the whole scope of human desire and human hope). Man lives ultimately in order to fulfill God's intention for his existence (whatever it might be) and man's religiosity causes him to look to God with all the force of his intelligence and freedom. For these reasons we can say that revelation (even while its specific content transcends man's nature and is therefore radically "un"-expected) also constitutes the *answer* to the wonder-filled, awesome, and intrinsically open *question* that constitutes the depths of human experience. In this essay we will examine the contours of this question, and the various ways that it emerges—clearly or obscurely—in the course of human life.

Intelligence and freedom are what distinguish man as a person. They are the foundational capacities that spring from, and therefore indicate, the heart of personal existence and its "super-material" character. Man "goes beyond" the physical universe (without thereby ceasing to be really present "within" it) in every genuine act of knowledge and love. In this way he manifests that his very being as a person is not limited and defined entirely by space and time, by parts and components.

Moreover, intelligence and freedom are capacities given by God to man so that man can recognize the true, the good, and the beautiful; so that man can be shaped in his personal existence by what is real, by what really exists, and so that he can direct his life in accordance with the full measure and significance of reality as indicative of the Mystery of God. Through his personal encounter with reality, man is capable of realizing that things are *signs* that "point toward" their Divine Source, Exemplar, and Goal. It is the Truth, Goodness, and Beauty of God that are reflected in things, and ultimately this is what truly fascinates man. At the same time the finite character of things highlights and impresses upon human awareness the *transcendence* of God. The Divine "Otherness" is precisely implied by the mystery of God's creative power and its all-encompassing character as Source of the very *being* of things.

At the height of the interaction between the human person and the realities of the world there is, therefore, this breathtakingly paradoxical experience: Man's fascination and desire are aimed at an Infinite Mystery—something he can neither comprehend nor possess by his own power. Moreover, when man turns from the realities of the world and looks "back" upon himself, he discovers that he too is rooted in the Mystery of God. He discovers that his own experience as a knowing and loving being has the character of a sign. The category of "sign," as was so well understood by St. Augustine and other great Christian thinkers, is particularly useful in attempting to understand the reality of creaturehood. Man's experience of the world and of himself reaches its summit in what can be called, by analogy, a "question." I mention analogy here because, although we can indicate this question terminologically, the following articulations scarcely exhaust the richness of the experience at hand, nor can they pretend to express it adequately. The question that man asks with his whole personal existence might be articulated in one of these ways: "What is the meaning of life?" "What is the ultimate purpose of things?" "What is the ultimately coherent story that makes everything fit together?" "Where does everything come from, and where is it going?" "Who is God?"

These questions correspond to man's being as an intelligent and free creature. The richness of a human person's experience will clarify the terms in which the question is asked; indeed the human search for meaning can lead man to levels of understanding which, *in a certain respect*, answer the question, at least in the sense that they bring man to a kind of plateau from which he glimpses an obscure view of its horizon. It is a great temptation for man to rest at one of the plateaus to which his intelligence is capable of climbing, and to be content with the view that it affords him. Each of these various vistas, however—whether they be the gaze on reality offered by natural science, or human psychology, or even by the heights of philosophy—opens up at the same time new dimensions of the inexhaustible search and new levels of its resonance within the person. This is because man's question is more than an informational question or even a speculative question. It is an existential question: man, if he realizes the truth of his created personhood by becoming aware of his dependence on God, ultimately desires to know and love in *some* fashion this Mysterious and Inexhaustible Knower and Lover who holds him in being. Naturally speaking, the rational and free created person can come to know and love his Creator as the Source of the being of all things, and especially as the Source of his own created personhood and that of others. Still, the created person recognizes that by his own inherent power he can only relate to the Creator "from a distance," so to speak. He is aware, however, that his relationship with his Creator has a certain "open-endedness" about it, and that his status before God ultimately depends upon God's design. This awareness, if it is genuine, knows that it possesses no "rights" in front of the Mystery of God or power to conjure a Divine response. Rather, it takes the form of a worshipful readiness, a hope that makes no claim nor pretense to deserve any further gift from the God who has already given to man his very being. And yet the being that God has created is a person—a knower and a lover—and therefore it cannot be itself if it does not ask in some fashion to know and love the Infinite

The Created Person and the Mystery of God

Personality that creates it.[1] Perhaps more appropriate that the term "question" as a description of the human experience of creaturehood would be the term "prayer." The summit of human creaturely existence is therefore *prayer* in the most basic sense.[2] It is a plea for the Mystery to have regard for man, to show something to man that will amplify his destiny, that will direct man on the road that his knowledge and love must take on this seemingly limitless journey toward the Infinite. This plea is not by nature desperate, but it is full of genuine desire. It proceeds not from any essential imperfection or defect in the structure of the created person, but precisely from its personal fullness.[3] It is the plea of created love for a word from Uncreated Love. It is, as St. Augustine indicates, an "emptiness" superior to any finite fullness, a longing for the Infinite that

---

[1] This is what Luigi Giussani means when he says that man's life is hunger and thirst for the Absolute. "Structurally man is a beggar." See *The Religious Sense* (Montreal: McGill-Queens, 1997), p. 54

[2] Theologically speaking, it is important to note that this "prayer" cannot in any way be said to "obtain" the free gift of supernatural grace, nor even to establish a "positive disposition" for it. In its inherent structure it is prayer for Divine Providence to lead man to his final end (thus, in theological terms, it merely pertains to the "obediential potency" of man to be raised to a supernatural level). Needless to say, however, the establishment of a supernatural finality for man and the gift of grace—even though they are not "obtained" by man as a simple response to the "prayer-structure" of his dependent and indigent creaturely existence—do in fact completely fulfill the human plea in that they contain in an eminent fashion everything that creaturely existence could ask for. Grace perfects nature. This is the basis for what we will refer to below as "correspondence."

[3] St. Thomas Aquinas indicates this when he says that it is more noble for a nature to desire something higher than itself, even if it requires help to attain it, than it is to merely desire something within its own power (see *Summa Theologiae* I-II, q. 5, a. 5, reply obj. 2).

An Essay in the Philosophy of Religion

is in itself sweeter and more satisfying than the possession of all finite things.[4] It waits upon the freedom of God.

This waiting shapes man's attitude toward life and suffuses all of his activity to the degree that he recognizes the mysterious truth that things in the world and even other created persons—with all of their charm, beauty, intricacy, and diverse riches and with all of their disappointing limits—are signs that point beyond themselves to the Infinite Beauty and Inexhaustible Fullness Who is their source. Thus for the mature man, for the wise man, an attitude of prayer, of poverty of spirit, of "waiting upon the Lord" radically defines the way he faces the whole of life even down to its humblest details. Every reality, for him, awakens, sustains, and deepens his fascination and reverence for the Divine Mystery and places him before that Mystery with open hands, with readiness to receive any Divine gift. This is the summit of human dignity: to wait upon the Lord.

Christians believe that God *has* indeed given to man an unimaginable gift: He has revealed and communicated Himself through Jesus to the human person who thus waits for Him. As we have already emphasized, the great plea

---

[4] St. Augustine emphasizes this theme and issues related to it in many places. For example in the *Confessions*, Book I, ch. 6, he says—with regard to the incomprehensible mystery of God—"I should like him too to rejoice [who] says [regarding God's eternity and simplicity]: 'What does this mean?' Yes; this is the way I should like him to rejoice, preferring to find you in his uncertainty rather than in his certainty to miss you." Man's openness to and acknowledgment of the mystery of God, even though it is experienced in the context of a "poverty of intellect" that is incapable of comprehending, is *a greater cause for joy* ("I should like him to *rejoice*") than all the things that man can comprehend by the measure of his own finite powers of knowledge.

that arises in the heart of the man who recognizes the truth of creation and the wonderful mystery of the Creator is not the *cause* of God's response, as though it made any claim on the freedom of God. Man's created spiritual and personal nature already attains an outstanding dignity in the recognition of the Mystery of God and in that poignant yearning for any manifestation of the beauty and love of that Mystery, in that "religious" attachment to the hint of God's presence contained in everything that is true and good, and in the continual disposition to follow the Divine Mystery—to ask for more, in every circumstance and in front of every thing, from the Giver of all gifts. Man's created nature certainly has no *right* to the superabundant gift that God has given to man in Jesus, which is nothing less than a share in the intimacy of His own Trinitarian life. What can be said, however, is this: If the "religious attitude"—the attitude of *prayer*—is the summit of the actualization of created personhood, then God's free decision to invite the created person into a *super*-natural participation in the Divine life *corresponds* to the depths of human existence in its natural structure and the openness of human existence to the design of Divine Wisdom and Love.

II. REALISM AND ANTHROPOCENTRISM

[1] General Considerations

Before we analyze further the openness of the human person in front of the mystery of God, we must examine two basic and architectonic attitudes which can ground the human person's approach to the world and to his own life. The first attitude, which we shall term the *realistic* attitude, leads to the growth and maturity of the human person. The second attitude, which we shall designate as the *anthropocentric* or "subjectivist" attitude, leads to the malformation of the person and tends to sap human life of its real vitality even while it claims to exalt the individual and his alleged dominance over reality and over his own decisions and purposes.

The realistic attitude can be defined as follows: truth and goodness are determined by the inherent intelligibility and value—the *real* meaning and purpose—of things in themselves, "independent" of my mind and will. My mind, will, and heart become conformed to the truth, goodness, and beauty inherent in reality insofar as I live with a realistic attitude. One can recall here the classical definition of truth as articulated by Thomas Aquinas: "truth is the conformity of the mind with reality."

The anthropocentric or subjectivist attitude, on the other hand, insists that the ultimate criterion for truth and goodness involves a coherence, a meaning, a purpose that somehow comes from within me and that I impose upon the phenomena of the external world, and—indeed—in the construction of my own "self-image."

Both of these attitudes can be articulated as epistemological positions, but it is important to note that they are first of all *attitudes toward life and toward one's own conception of one's self.* If we consider realism and anthropocentrism as practical attitudes, it should be quite apparent that realism is the natural human "position" in the face of life. Psychologically speaking, realism corresponds to a healthy human attitude; and it is ordinarily the attitude that we "naturally" take up from the moment we open our eyes in the morning. Practical examples abound: when we are hungry we eat bread and not stones; when we are thirsty we drink water and not gasoline. We must satisfy our basic human needs with the things that correspond to them—not, obviously, with the things that oppose them. Our practical need to live according to "the way things really are" is evident. This is so much the case that, clearly, the anthropocentric attitude would be understood as a psychological disorder and a moral malaise if we observed it being applied to the most mundane matters of life. If we saw a person put a gasoline nozzle to his mouth and start drinking, we would be instinctively stricken with a sense of panic and with the urgent desire to stop the person from poisoning himself. And if he responded to our efforts by saying, "I am an autonomous individual who has the right to decide for myself the meaning and value of things, and I have freely chosen to drink gasoline because I have determined that this is what gasoline means for me personally," we would—hopefully—be neither convinced nor dissuaded in our efforts to stop him from killing himself.

Having noted the diversity between these attitudes in very simple terms, we must then observe with great dismay

An Essay in the Philosophy of Religion

the fact that the anthropocentric attitude is becoming more and more pervasive in our culture, first and foremost in the delicate realm of the inner life of the person where its violence and destructiveness are not easily perceived by others or even by the person himself. A particularly disturbing illustration of this can be found in a statement from a recent United States Supreme Court decision: "every human person has the right to decide for himself the meaning of the universe, of existence, and of the purposes of his own life."[5] This statement is not merely emblematic of the grave moral disorder that pervades our society; it is a profound error of *perception*—indeed, it is a much more profound failure *to see things as they really are* than the hypothetical case of the man drinking gasoline.

The truth is that this anthropocentric mentality enters into human judgments and human perceptions about life insofar as people are tempted either to take pride in their own power or to rationalize in order to avoid the objective truth about something. More and more we live in a culture in which pride in human power and the rationalization of human whims have become the governing forces that shape the common mentality. This is the real basis of what Pope John Paul II calls "the culture of death." Luigi Giussani has fundamentally the same thing in mind when he refers to "the culture of original sin"—which means that the weakness and disorder identified by the Christian tradition as rooted in *original sin* are not only present and operative among us, but they are being exalted as the *model* of human life.

---

[5] See the text of the majority report of the Supreme Court Decision *Casey vs. Reproductive Health Services* (1993).

Any claim about God and the great merciful events of His incarnation and redemption becomes very difficult to propose in such a social milieu. Realism is the presupposition for Christianity (19th and 20th century attempts to rearticulate the Christian faith in terms of the subjectivist mentality, while often being theoretically impressive, have all failed to reinvigorate the Christian faith in the contemporary world). A realist attitude affects in a very basic way how we approach questions in life and evaluate things. Realism looks at a thing according to every aspect that it "evinces." Realism seeks constantly for and attends to the evidence that the thing itself presents regarding the thing's own inherent significance and value. A realist does not, therefore, bend the evidence manifested by things and situations within the circumstances of life in order to support his ideology or his subjective desires. He does not ignore pieces of evidence that contradict his pre-established view or wish about how something ought to be. Because he is interested in the objective truth that is indicated and manifested by things, he is willing to *follow* these indications, to discover new truths, to have his vision of reality increased and deepened. And because he is obedient to the truth, he will embrace the truth that is thus manifested to him even if it seems inconvenient or makes demands upon him. He will not try to rationalize, explain away, or ignore anything that is made clear to him by the evidence. He will embrace the conclusion that follows naturally from the evidence rather than exaggerating the importance of unessential points that perhaps remain obscure in order to have a pretext for *evading* this conclusion.

Many people might still agree today that the realist attitude described above represents the ideal for how a human being ought to live his daily life. Nevertheless, it is singularly difficult for many people today, especially in the affluent West, to be genuinely realistic in their attitude in front of anything that might require them to *change their way of behaving*. Certainly it is always difficult for frail human nature to accept the challenge of personal (i.e. moral) maturity. The realistic attitude about man is richly aware of the fact that man is a sinner, and that his personal resources are fragile and in need of both internal and external supports. The problem today, however, is made much more acute by the fact that people today are systematically mis-educated in the anthropocentric attitude and in the pride and rationalization that go with it. We are taught and are surrounded by a culture that constantly impresses upon us the idea that our human fragility is actually strength, our foolishness is wisdom, our instinctual whims are genuine judgments regarding what is good. Moreover, this attitude reigns almost without opposition in the highest realms of human perception, namely the realms of ontology and religion, where man must grapple with the most fundamental truths about the world and about his own personality.

Nevertheless, some aspects of the attitude of realism remain alive in any person who possesses any measure of sanity. Human beings by nature are so "attuned" to reality that even the subjectivist, anthropocentric attitude cannot assert itself as a social proposal by appealing to raw selfishness. Rather, anthropocentrism inevitably seeks to *justify* itself theoretically—in other words, to say, "it is *objectively true* (i.e. it is proper to the objective reality of how man's intellect and will operate) that man determine for himself the meaning of things." This implies that there is at least one thing that man does not determine for himself, namely, his power to determine the ultimate significance of everything for himself. This power is universal; it is the "right" of every man, and indeed a "given" of human existence. Thus even anthropocentrism is led inexorably to give some *objective* account of the nature of the human person.

The simple fact is that realism is inherent to the very nature of thinking—so much so that no one feels comfortable with a radical and total skepticism. Certitudes of some kind need to be discovered or the human being begins to suffocate. What predominates in our culture is a *selective* skepticism about the possibility of universal certitudes about certain facets of reality. Since the scope of this essay is not primarily epistemological, we can do no more than mention the fact that such selective skepticism inevitably "cheats" intellectually. The famous example of the problem of logical positivism should suffice to illustrate this for us. The assertion, "nothing is meaningful except what can be empirically verified" is a meta-empirical assertion; not only is the statement itself impossible to verify empirically (thus breaking its own rule), it is in fact an ontological statement. It presupposes transempirical ideals of meaningfulness and verifiability that would never even occur to a person whose modes of perception were entirely confined to sense experience and cognition.[6]

---

[6] For a thorough analysis of "critical realism" see Jacques Maritain, *The Degrees of Knowledge*, trans. G. B. Phelan et. al. (New York: Charles Scribner's Sons, 1959), pp. 72-75.

An Essay in the Philosophy of Religion

The truth of the realistic attitude is, simply, *evident*; it is at the basis of all our thinking. We would be wise to heed the advice of Aristotle that only the foolish man demands proof of the obvious. We must not, therefore, try to prove realism by starting out from the premise that realism is somehow not evident. This is a deadly trap for the human mind. Rather the way to overcome the subjectivist attitude is to bear witness to realism in our own lives. Our contemporaries—no matter what their theories may be, no matter what psychological tricks they may play—are human beings who have been created to hunger and thirst for truth, goodness, and beauty. If you live in front of them, day after day, with a sense of wonder in the presence of things, a sense of the givenness of things, an openness to learn, a willingness to transcend your own selfishness and be shaped by a design for your life that is not ultimately determined by you, but is given to you through the truth of the circumstances you face every day—if you live like this, they will recognize in you the truth about themselves, about the attitude that a human being needs in order to be truly human, that is, to be *happy*. The answer to the oppressiveness of the culture of death is to begin to build within our own lives the culture of life, the culture of realism. Within the context of this witness and of its attractive force, the people we meet may be willing to take the risk of facing reality and of opening up their own lives to its mysterious design.

Let us now clarify further a few basic points of the epistemological expression of these two attitudes.

[2] Epistemological Reflections

(i) Realist Epistemology

A realist epistemology is based on two fundamental convictions: (1) The reliability of the senses—things in the world manifest their particular characteristics to us through the senses; (2) The mind's capacity to perceive universal truths about things. In the latter case what we are talking about is not simply the mind grouping particular sense perceptions into broader and more general classifications. Rather, we are referring to the mind's trans-sensational power to *draw out* those features of a thing that go beyond its sensed particularity and pertain to its intelligible significance, and then to express, by means of a "mental visualization"[7], the coherent and interrelated complex of these features. To put it more simply, the mind has the power to form concepts of "what things are"—things that enter the milieu of human experience by means of the senses.

There is a corollary to this point that is very important to stress: realistic knowledge does not *begin* with an analysis of the thinking process itself (i.e. with Descartes's "cogito"). Rather, knowledge begins with the encounter with reality manifested to the senses and grasped in its intelligible features by the mind. It is only because I have *already* been thinking about the realities outside myself that I can then "turn toward myself," so to speak, and make this thinking process an object of analysis. As we shall explore

---

[7] This perhaps awkward phrase owes something to Maritain's attempt to translate that classical Thomistic notion of *abstractio formalis* in a manner that is free from the intellectual baggage that modern epistemology has heaped upon the term "abstraction."

in greater detail, it is this realist *openness* of the human mind that allows the things around me to disclose—by their very complexity, variation, harmonious purposefulness and inner splendor—their intrinsic relationship to the mysterious Source that creates and sustains them. And we shall also see that it is the same realism that enables me to look at the wonder of my own self and be led to the recognition of my fundamental dependence on that very same mysterious Other. Epistemological realism leads man to certain convictions about metaphysics (i.e. that the things he perceives in the physical world are rooted in Something and point toward Something that transcends the physical world) and about what Hans Urs Von Balthasar has referred to as "meta-anthropology"[8] (i.e. that man *is himself* because he comes from and is called to Another, because he *belongs*—not as property but in the deepest interpersonal sense—to this Other).

---

[8] Von Balthasar deals with this theme in particular detail in the second volume of the *Theodramatik*. Ellero Babini synthesizes the point that man is himself and becomes more fully himself through transcendence toward his Divine Creator and Destiny: "man is a being in the process of becoming (to use biblical language, he is an *image* of God destined for an ever fuller *likeness* to him...)" Babini notes that, for Von Balthasar, "man as such in his creatureliness" is "a response to the God who has created him" and who gives him a calling, a vocation, a *mission* (this latter term is fundamental to Von Balthasar's theological anthropology). "By means of the mission received, man discovers why he has been made and who he really is, since it is in mission, received as gift from an 'other,' that he hears himself called as an 'I' by a 'Thou' and (made responsible by this latter) called to a response. The responsibility (which engages the freedom of the person, and in which the human subject reaches maturation and arrives at his adult stature) is responsibility for a charge, for a mission received, for a work which involves and is inseparable from the person's whole existence." See Ellero Babini, "Jesus Christ, form and norm of man according to Hans Urs Von Balthasar," *Communio* 16 (Fall 1989), pp. 447-448.

(ii) Anthropocentric Epistemologies

The anthropocentric attitude is expressed in various epistemological theories. We will mention two broad categories that are most common and influential, keeping in mind that the various philosophical positions that fall under these categories have various nuances.

[1] Rationalism/Idealism: Knowledge is the activity of the mind producing objects of thought (ideas), organizing them, and reflecting upon them. Idealism says that we do not know, however, whether this mental process conforms to anything beyond the phenomena of our consciousness and its activities. Some forms of idealism say that the realities "outside" our mind are "really there" but are not directly knowable in themselves (Kant). Other forms of idealism say that there are no meaningful, intelligible realities independent of the mind. Reality—insofar as it has any significance—is constituted by *thought process* itself. It is probably inadequate to summarize the great philosophical synthesis of Hegel in such superficial terms; nevertheless this appears to be the core of his position, along with the theory that our little, individual thought processes are aspects or historical moments of the Great Absolute Thought Process as it unfolds itself within the Trancendental Mind.

The philosophical problems with this position are rooted in the basic starting point taken up by Descartes as well as his account of the role of the idea in knowledge. The plain fact is that our ordinary experience of human knowing simply does not correspond to the account given by the Cartesian model, which is more and more admitted even by many "post-modern" philosophers who have little or no interest in classical epistemology. Human knowledge is not a process of generating ideas as expressions of one's own mind and then looking at those ideas and analyzing their content. The intelligible characteristics of a thing, the meaningfulness inherent in a thing, is what engages the mind and draws forth its potentiality for knowledge. The idea is the *means through which* the mind reaches forth to grasp and to "live intentionally" (as Maritain would say[9]) the real significance inherent in some thing. The great mistake of idealism is to say that *what* we know are our ideas; in fact what we know are the intelligible features of reality *by means of* ideas, or better, *concepts*.[10]

Rationalist idealism is tempting nevertheless, not only because it offers an apparently rich path for the mind's magnanimous appetite for notional systematization, but also because what ultimately underlies it is the supposition that the human mind is *sufficient unto itself,* that it does not need to submit itself to reality and be shaped by the real in all of its complexity. It proposes that the mind need only affirm and express itself and unfold its own inner logic.[11] Idealism, in the modern world, has been the vehicle of a great mental

---

[9] See on this point Maritain, *Bergsonian Philosophy and Thomism*, trans. Mabelle L. Andison and J. Gordon Andison (New York: Philosophical Library, 1955), p. 104, pp. 150-151. See also Maritain, *The Degrees of Knowledge*, p. 113.

[10] This latter term more accurately conveys the fact that the mind receives the *logos spermatikos* (the "seed of potential intelligibility," that Augustine and other early Christian writers make reference to) of a thing into itself and "conceives" within itself an image, a *sign* that has its source in the thing and that establishes a real relationship between the mind and the thing it perceives.

[11] Let us not forget that this was Descartes's great ambition: to establish a universal science that was easy and accessible to anyone.

hubris, a pride of intellect in which man seeks to be the source of truth rather than *obedient* to the truth.

[2] Empiricism/Positivism. The Positivist position, unlike idealism, does hold that knowledge consists in some fashion of a correspondence between the mind and reality. However, it asserts that the only kind of serious knowledge—wherein mind deals with reality in a significant way—is the knowledge of facts gained from sense experience, and classifications and generalizations drawn from these facts. Real knowledge therefore, according to this position, consists in the data, analysis, and organizational schemes of the empirical sciences. The height of human reason is achieved in empirical science.[12] Therefore metaphysics and theology, religion and moral thinking—because they do not deal with empirically verifiable schemes—are not reasonable activities, but at best hypothetical assertions that can never be "proved" (i.e. tested), or else expressions of psychological states, emotional needs, or even mental pathologies.

Positivism is probably more dominant than idealism as a generally accepted theory of knowledge in our present culture. Indeed, this view usually calls itself "realism" because it claims to stick strictly to the objective facts. The

---

[12] It is worth noting that the triumph of this prejudice in the common mentality of our culture is so complete that we use the word "science" exclusively with reference to the empirical sciences. The classical latin term *scientia*, by contrast, referred to the whole realm of demonstrable knowledge, including the various branches of philosophy crowned by metaphysics. For medieval Catholic thinkers, theology was the highest science, and the Blessed in heaven who knew God face to face were said to possess the "scientia beatifica." All of this, needless to say, is meaningless to the positivist mentality, which conceives of anything beyond the empirically verifiable as belonging to the realm of irresolvable opinion.

truth is, however, that this position looks at *only a portion* of reality and systematically excludes other facets of reality from the realm of knowledge. Ultimately its objectivity is a pretense, because the criteria by which it determines what ought to be looked at are not "objective" at all. Positivism essentially holds that reason is limited to what Maritain calls "empiriological analysis." It denies reason's capacity for "ontological analysis."[13] So positivism accepts (more or less) the reliability of the senses, but it views the intellect as nothing more than a kind of processor of sense information, organizing and classifying and then returning to physically measured facts in order to see if these organizational schemes "fit"—usually the aim is practical: the intellect schematizes in order to *dominate* physical reality, to uncover its laws of operation, predict what it will do, manipulate it so that it will do things that we want it to do. All of this is fine as far as it goes. This kind of intellectual analysis is what the empirical sciences do best, and it is responsible for the incredible advances of the modern world in understanding how the physical universe "works" and in meeting various human needs through technology. But all of this success does not justify the conclusion that the empirical scientific method is the *only way that reason works*!

It has already been pointed out that positivism is ultimately self-refuting as a theoretical position, since it must make an ontological affirmation (an affirmation about what knowledge *is*, and what it *is not*) in order to deny the possibility of making ontological affirmations. The

---

[13] For a thorough account of this distinction, see Maritain, *Degrees of Knowledge*, pp. 146-148.

frustrating and indeed distressing fact, however, is that it is not uncommon to observe very intelligent people (even trained scientists) who are so immersed in a mindset equating knowledge with empirical verification and practical power that they simply *don't care* about the theoretical incoherence of their epistemological position. They assert their first principle because it is practical and workable. Press them a little, however, and they may begin to claim that scientific advances have improved the lot of humanity and delivered us from "the dark ages" and witch hunts and superstitions and other bad things. We thus begin to discover that the positivist has other meta-empirical convictions—after all, humanity's "improvement" can only be gauged according to some criteria for determining *the good*.

It cannot be denied, however, that what holds the modern mentality in thralldom to the ideology of positivist science is its spectacular success in expanding man's *power*. Our world is still intoxicated with the fantastic success of science and technology, and the immediately perceivable *usefulness* of this type of knowledge. Contemporary man's preoccupation with his power over the external and the material has led him to neglect the higher realms of intellectual wisdom and the truths that pertain to his own inner life. If religion has any role in the positivist world, it is not because it can make any appeal to objective truth or to man's reason, but only because it may be *useful* in fulfilling psychological or emotional needs. In this way, religion might perhaps assist in the manipulation and management of that curious and still not fully understood fact of the universe classified as *homo sapiens*.[14]

In light of all this, we must conclude that positivism—in spite of its pretenses of being "realist"—ultimately measures the meaningfulness and the value of things according to the scope of man's power over the things that he can observe, calculate, and organize—thereby rendering them subject to his use. Since this power of man is great, the positivist mentality appears increasingly convincing and adequate as it achieves greater and greater material success. It is nevertheless an "anthropocentric" position rather than a realist position, because it refuses to give attention to any aspect of reality that cannot be subjected to man—that, indeed, might even be greater than man.

The fact is, however, that there is no rational basis for the positivist denial that we can *know* the truth about realities that transcend the realm of empirical verifiability: realities such as the human soul, metaphysical principles, or God. It follows that there is no reason for relegating religion to the margins of human existence, as a mere idiosyncrasy, emotional crutch, or expression of some psychological need that empirical science has not yet fully analyzed. The positivist position, insofar as it has pervaded our culture, has deformed and crippled the human person; it puts a tight lid on the rising steam of the aspiration of the human spirit, hoping thereby to harness all the boiling energy of man's desire to cook its own stew inside the pot.

---

[14] It is intriguing that man's biological species classification includes a reference to *sapientia* or wisdom, although there are some who would like to refer to man as *homo faber*—seeing his specification in his ability to make things or even to use tools. Thus man would be reduced to one of his external functions.

Any cook knows (and any positivistic scientist should also know) that sooner or later the lid will blow off and the pot will boil over. Perhaps one may be permitted to speculate that the internal and external violence and barbarism so prevalent and so much on the increase in our time are in part an uncontrolled reaction to the suffocating constriction imposed upon the human person by the mentality of the 20th century. In any case, positivism has blocked man from the discovery that the dignity of his intelligence and his freedom reaches its summit in an encounter with reality and an understanding of himself that is pervaded by a *religious* awareness.

III. THE EXISTENCE OF GOD

"For what can be known about God is plain to them, because God has shown it to them. Ever since the creation of the world his invisible nature, namely, his eternal power and deity, has been clearly perceived in the things that have been made" (Rom 1:19-20).

[1] "Ways" to God in St. Thomas Aquinas

We have seen the need for realism as the adequate approach of the human person to knowing and loving other persons and things and indeed his very self. It is the lived practice of such a realism that will lead the human person to the conviction that things are created, and that he—the person—is a creature. The fundamental human posture of realism is the presupposition of St. Paul's text from Romans 1, and indeed for the whole human discovery of God. The great 20th century French Catholic philosopher Jacques Maritain comments that St. Paul is referring not only (or even primarily) to philosophic proofs drawn from speculative metaphysics but also and first of all to "the natural ['prephilosophic'] knowledge of the existence of God to which the vision of created things leads the reason of every man, philosopher or not."[15] Maritain points out that St. Thomas's five ways of proving the existence of God are scientifically elaborated and clarified arguments that

---

[15] Jacques Maritain, *Approaches to God* (New York: Harper, 1954), p. 4.

unfold the logic implicitly present in a more concrete reasoning process—a process that is possible for anyone who honestly and openly approaches the world of reality.

Maritain points specifically to the basic human perception of the contingency of things and the contingency of one's own self. We have already alluded to the natural conviction of the reality of things that is at the beginning of our knowledge. "Something exists," "things exist," this thing, that thing. Existence strikes my intellect in a such a fundamental and compelling way that the basic conviction of the being of things is firm and unassailable for any intelligence not caught in a moral quagmire or neurotic paralysis. At the same time, although "existing" strikes me as so solid, the existence of this or that thing—considered simply as contained within its individual being—seems completely fragile; indeed the more we ponder it, the more inexplicable it seems to be.[16]

Contingency—why is it that anything exists at all? All the stuff around us doesn't seem to do justice to the monumental solidity of "existence" as it impresses itself upon even common sense human reasoning. As a result, there is the natural human question, as old as the human race itself, the question that every civilization tries to answer and that every man—in his own way—tries to answer: "what's 'behind' all of this?" "Where did it all

---

16 This fragility of things in their "own" being has been deeply pondered by some of the existentialists of the twentieth century and has given rise to notions of *angst* (Heidegger) and *nausea* (Sartre) that are not to be taken lightly. Indeed such notions are full of metaphysical density precisely because they approach, in a certain respect, the core of the mystery of created being but nevertheless miss the mark and thus—by a kind of ontological centrifugal force—they are thrown far afield.

come from?" These things I see and hear and touch and think about—these things exist, but they are not responsible for their own existence and they can't keep themselves in existence. They must exist *on account of something else.* Thus even ordinary day-to-day human thinking, when it is open to reality, can arrive at the perception of the *contingency* of things and of their *dependence.* Common sense can therefore arrive at a fundamental notion of things as creatures. This notion is not philosophically clarified in the mind of the average person, but it is capable of being both powerful and convincing on an existential level.

In the same way, the natural down-to-earth movements of human reason in front of reality perceive that things are *changeable* (they become what they were not before); that situations do not just spring up without antecedent factors bringing them about (i.e. that *effects proceed from causes*), that there is a hierarchical character to the perfections of beings, and that beings possess an inherent intelligibility and purposefulness.

Indeed, the proofs that St. Thomas advances in the *Summa Theologiae* I, q. 3, a. 2 are really philosophical demonstrations that render in a clear, consistent, and logically coherent manner the "ways" that the mind and heart of every human person can come to a practical and firm conviction about the existence of God. The human person should be led "upward" by means of his normal intercourse with the world of created things and his normal re-flection upon the himself engaging and acting within that world. If he is truly attentive to reality and to himself, he will at least begin to be aware that there is Something Else present to everything as its Mysterious Source and sustenance.[17]

The classical philosophical arguments of Aquinas, indeed, are usually only convincing to the person whose reason and freedom function with a childlike openness and simplicity. It is (surprisingly, perhaps) only through the uncomplicated gaze of a genuine and honest realism that human beings can begin to perceive the contingent, caused, changeable, valuable, intelligible and purposeful character of things in the world, and thus be led to the affirmation of the necessary Being who is primary cause, origin of all change, summit of all perfection, and final reason for which all things act.[18]

There is a great deal of philosophical debate (and always has been) about the demonstrative value of the famous "five ways" of St. Thomas Aquinas for proving the existence of God.[19] There is even disagreement among philosophers over Aquinas's precise method and intent in proposing these "ways." Nevertheless, none of this need prevent us

---

[17] See especially on this point Luigi Giussani, *The Religious Sense*. pp. 99-109.

[18] Every human being has this uncomplicated attitude on at least some level. It usually manifests itself in the ordinary certainties that constitute the fabric of life. Relativists make absolute statements in the name of absolute values. Materialists and behaviorists fall in love. Even the ideological atheist who will assert that the apparent intelligibility of things is a mere random coalescence of elements will tell you that you are crazy if you say that the book on atheism he is reading is a mere random arrangement of ink stains. The argument of the book obviously points to an intelligent "arguer" who wrote it. Why, then, is the atheist content to assert that the great argument of the universe is nothing more than a happy coincidence of elements?

[19] *Summa Theologiae* I, q. 2, a. 3.

from appreciating the argumentative force of the five ways in terms of their conceptual clarification of how man perceives things in the world and reasons from them to the existence of the God who creates, sustains, designs, and governs the world. Briefly, Aquinas proposes his "five ways" as follows:

(1) "Whatever is in motion is put in motion by another...therefore it is necessary to arrive at a First Mover." We should note that for Aquinas the ontological factor of "motion" has a much broader sense than what we understand as "local motion"—the movement of physical objects from one place to another—even though Aquinas viewed local motion as an easily perceived and therefore accessible example of *motio*. The force of the term "motio" in this argument, however, can only be appreciated if we realize that Aquinas is using it to refer to the whole mysterious phenomenon of *change*, the actualization of potential, the realization of some capacity. When something "moves" in this sense, it *becomes* in some respect what it wasn't before.

(2) The order of efficient causes requires a First Efficient Cause.

(3) Realities in the world are contingent; they don't *have* to exist, and the only thing that explains why they exist at all is that there is some necessary being.

(4) The varying degrees of goodness, truth, and nobility in things leads us to affirm a maximum—a definitive goodness, truth, and nobility which causes all perfections in things, and against which everything else is measured.

(5) The governance of all things toward intelligent purposes proves that "some intelligent being exists by whom all natural things are directed to their end."

Thus, St. Thomas arrives, respectively, at a First Mover, First Efficient Cause, Necessary Being, Cause of all Perfection, and Intelligent Governor of the Universe; and at the conclusion of each proof he notes that "this being we call God" or "this everyone understands to be God."

What is particularly interesting about these proofs, however (and is, indeed, perhaps the key to their significance), is *how they start off*. Number 1: "It is certain, and *evident to our senses*, that in the world some things are in motion." Number 2: "*In the world of sense* we find that there is an order of efficient causes." Number 3: "*We find in nature* things that are possible to be and not to be, since they are found to be generated and to corrupt." Number 4: "The fourth way is taken from the gradation *to be found in things*." Number 5: "*We see that things* which lack intelligence, such as natural bodies, act for an end."

In other words, Aquinas's proofs begin with the ordinary things of this world, as they are accessible to everyone: the ordinary things that we see, hear, and touch with our senses, and analyze through our normal reasoning processes. A basic point underlying St. Thomas's five ways is that we are led to recognize the existence of God by all of the realities that we come into contact with in our ordinary human experience. The things that surround us and engage us through our senses are *effects*, and if we really pay attention to these effects we will be led by them to their Cause.

It is worth dwelling for a moment on what transpires in the cause-effect relationship. Causality is a metaphysical mystery: one being moves another being from potentiality to actuality in a certain respect, with regard to a certain perfection which the mover possesses and the moved does not yet possess, but receives a share in as a result of the action of the cause. Causality is therefore something much more profound than just a "mechanistic push;" it is an ontological communication, an influx of reality, of realization—it involves a kind of "metaphysical gift" in the interaction between one being and another; and the effect—by participating in the perfection of the cause—receives, so to speak, the "signature" of the cause upon itself.

Thus, the various features that we can recognize about all the things that we see, hear, and touch—the fact that they are changeable, that they are contingent, that they each possess a certain real but limited value, that they are ordered toward wise purposes—all of these features indicate that the things of this world are *effects*, that they are *made*, that they are creatures and that therefore there must be a Creator. Aquinas's proofs are different articulations of the fundamental fact that the things we see, hear, and touch cannot give an adequate account of themselves and their own characteristics. The visible things of this world point toward their invisible source.

The five "ways," however, are not the only arguments St. Thomas makes for the existence of God. In a small early treatise entitled *De Ente et Essentia*, St. Thomas proposes an argument for the existence of God which takes as its starting point not the various activities and characteristics of created things, but their most fundamental "activity"—their very act of existing. In chapter five of *De Ente et Essentia*, Thomas argues that, with regard to all of the things that we encounter, "what they are" cannot explain the *fact that they actually do exist* in reality. Therefore their existence must be explained in terms of *Something Else*; it must be *caused* by Something Else.

The main principle that St. Thomas develops in this little treatise is that there is a real distinction between essence and existence, between the integrated complexus of specifications that define *what* something is, and the *actualization* of that specificity, the "placing" of it into the real universe of existence.

The existing of something—its *esse* (to use the Latin infinitive for the verb "to be"), the act by which it "is"—is distinct from "what it is," its *essence*. Existing introduces another dimension beyond everything we can say about *what* a thing is. When I say "the horse exists," I take the whole richly envisioned description of "horse" that I an able to apprehend and examine with my mind, *and I affirm "something else"* with regard to the horse, something that is not part of the description of a horse; I judge an instance of this essence (the "whatness" of horse—"horseness") to be *there* in reality. The horse *is*. The horse is *existing*.

Notice something very important here: *existing is an act*. It is the most fundamental of all acts. To exist is dynamic, *radically* dynamic. The reason why we think of existing as static is because we are surrounded by it everywhere and therefore inclined to take it for granted. But things are not just plopped around us—just "there," with this fact worthy of nothing more than a "ho-hum" from our faculties of perception. On the contrary, things are bursting with being. "Is-ing" is a fascinating and powerful achievement—the achievement of *really existing* which should never be taken simply as a given, as something that does not provoke our minds to wonder.[20] We have allowed ourselves to be lulled into metaphysical sleep by the apparently commonplace character of the existence of things. We must realize, instead, that the existing of any thing is a spectacular and awe-inspiring *event*.

This realization, achieved by means of a sufficiently intense attention to the reality of things, will lead us to recognize that existing is an actualization that comes to an essence "from outside." It is at one and the same time *the fundamental act* that any thing "does," and an act that does not emerge from a thing's own essential power, and which therefore must be brought about in it by Something Else. When we say "John runs," we recognize that "running" is an activity distinct from "John"—something that John does; John "actualized" in a certain respect, John moving from one place to another. However, this act takes place as a result of John's own inherent capacities: he causes himself to run by means of the muscular energy he possesses by virtue of the organic and "animal" characteristics that are proper features of his essence.

When we say "John exists," however, we are talking about *the* fundamental actualization of John. Could John be the cause of his own existence? It is not possible. In order to bring about an effect, a cause has to "be there," but John without the act of existing *is not* "*there*," and therefore he cannot bring about any effect at all, much less his own existence.

---

[20] This point was constantly stressed by the twentieth century American Existential Thomist philosopher Frederick Wilhelmsen, who saw it as the cornerstone of Thomistic metaphysics.

So how is it, then, that John exercises the act of existing? He must receive the impetus of this act from some outside source. At this point in the argument, St. Thomas invokes the principle that there cannot be an infinite series of caused causes, and thus concludes that there must be a *First Cause* that gives to all other things their act of existing. As First Cause, it is the Origin of all existence, which means that it does not receive its act of existing from anywhere else—it possesses "existing" properly, as the very definition of what it is. Its essence is "to exist;" it is *Sheer Existence*, the subsistent, pure act of "to be." This Being, indeed, is the Being we call God.

To summarize the argument in simple terms: Our existence does not come from ourselves; it is *given* to us. This means that there must be a *Giver* of existence who is the Source of this gift, who therefore possesses it essentially and fully. We *have* existence because we receive it from the One who *is* Existence—Pure and Absolute Existence.

One will generally find, however, that educated members of our culture dominated by the positivist mentality will object to the assertion that there cannot be an infinite series of caused causes. It is interesting to observe that for the ancient and medieval mind this assertion was one of those obvious statements for which an argument did not even seem necessary. The reason for this is not pre-modern scientific naiveté, but a living awareness of what we referred to above as the metaphysical mystery of causality. This awareness has largely disappeared from the contemporary cultural mentality due to the totalitarian pretenses of empirical analysis. We are incapable of perceiving the cause-effect relationship "from the inside" (so to speak) as an ontological communication of being and

An Essay in the Philosophy of Religion

activity. Instead we have reduced causality to the extrinsic, empirical observation of a sequence. Ever since Hume, the modern mentality has tended to assume that the human mind, trapped within the limits of empirical analysis, can only verify the extrinsic connection between a given series of factors and the subsequent event or events that are regularly observed to follow from them. Then, since we can imagine (or at least we *think* we can imagine) such an extrinsic sequence stretching back infinitely into the past, we conclude that an infinite series of caused causes is possible.

If, however, we appreciated the fact that an ontological reality is being *transmitted* from cause to effect, then we would easily realize that there must be a *source* of the reality that is being transmitted. Once again the point is rather easily illustrated by an appeal to common sense: if we see a series of train cars moving along a track, we are certain that there is an engine car at the beginning. There is a "pulling energy" being transmitted from one car to the next, but that energy has to come from some source; it has to "start" somewhere.

Another objection that is sometimes raised by otherwise intelligent people today goes something like this: "there is no explanation for the existence of things—they just exist! Existence is just a self-evident, presupposed starting point. Things are just there, and that is all we can say about existence." This is not an intelligibly defensible position, however. It is not a position worthy of the nobility and urgency of human curiosity. Rather, we must not be afraid to call it what it is: a cop-out. It is a strange and sad thing that minds otherwise possessed of such a high level of scientific integrity should resort to such a cheap evasion in front of the most interesting question in the whole universe. In a world that everywhere reveals its order and intelligibility are we to believe that the most fundamental fact—the existence of things—has no explanation, nothing that accounts for it? Human reason cannot be satisfied with such an irrational postulate, unless it gives in to intellectual laziness, or unless it stubbornly refuses to give up the prejudices of the positivistic method. The real reason why many adopt such a position is that they recognize that the empirical sciences cannot answer the question of why things exist; therefore, since they refuse to admit that anything can be understood beyond the scope of empirical analysis, they are forced to conclude that *there simply is no answer* to such a question. However, this is not seeking truth, but simply ending the investigation without any justification.

Indeed, an honest scientist should be able to realize that he has no justification for evading this question. He should consider a case within the scope of his own proper methodology: what would he think of an astronomer who has a telescope of limited power, who—looking out at the sky—notes down all the observations he is capable of making but simply dismisses as uninteresting or unobservable anything that eludes his telescope's capacities? Or, perhaps the astronomer cites a mysterious fuzzy ball, fainter in his view than the stars that appear clearly to him. Would it be appropriate for him to conclude his investigation by announcing that "I have discovered that there are faint, fuzzy balls in the universe?" What scientist would not consider such an astronomer to be irresponsible in making such dismissals and crass assertions? At the very least, the astronomer should admit that there are many things that his limited instrument is incapable of perceiving clearly. Better still, he should seek to obtain a more powerful telescope. So also should it be for the question: "why do the stars exist?" No one is justified in dismissing this question or giving up on it simply because the mental telescope of empirical astronomy is not powerful enough to focus on the answer.

[2] Attempts to Arrive at God's Existence Through a Direct Intra-subjective Idea or Experience

In proposing the "five ways," in the *Summa*, St. Thomas alludes to two types of demonstration: *propter quid* and *quia*. These scholastic terms are often indicated in broader philosophical discussion by the expressions "*a-priori*" and "*a-posteriori*."[21] An *a-priori* demonstration argues from cause to the effects implied by the operation of that cause. It begins with what is "prior" metaphysically speaking, and uses reasoning to come to a knowledge of how a reality that I already know brings about something else. An *a-posteriori* demonstration argues from effects to the cause that must be responsible for them. Here, although we begin by what is "prior" in our experience, we are actually examining what is "posterior" ontologically speaking. First we see some effects, and by analyzing them we demonstrate their cause. This is possible because a cause transmits something of its own actuality and perfection to its effect and—so to speak—leaves its "imprint" upon it.

---

[21] *Summa Theologiae* I, q. 2, a. 2.

This distinction between *a-priori* and *a-posteriori* demonstrations leads us to consider one of the most famous questions in the whole history of philosophy: Is an *a-priori* proof for the existence of God possible? Such a proof would require us to know in some way the reality that causes the beings of the universe "prior" to (or at least independently of) the consideration of its effects, i.e. things in the real world. Modern philosophers in particular have experimented and attempted in various ways to formulate an *a-priori* proof for the existence of God. Usually, it requires them to posit some idea about God implanted in our minds immediately and naturally, "before" our mind encounters the world of beings. They posit that the *idea* of God as First Cause and Infinite Perfection or as "Absolute" or as "Primal Reality upon whom I utterly depend" is somehow either *given* as part of the very structure of the mind or else it emerges spontaneously as soon as the mind begins to think. The idea of God, according to such a position, is an *innate idea*, and in order to appreciate the underlying thrust of such a proposal we must take seriously both of the terms involved in this complex concept. It is "innate," which means that it is inborn within us in an *actual* form, as part of the knowing process itself. As "idea," what is usually intended is a fully or at least substantially formed apprehension of God's existence that is self verifying and can be examined by the knowing subject without drawing on the evidence of anything perceived from the outside world. For reasons that we will examine further below, the philosophical project of establishing God's existence *a-priori* has never succeeded

An Essay in the Philosophy of Religion

in convincing many people.[22] Yet it continues—in various forms—to capture the imagination of philosophers and religious thinkers. Why is this?

---

[22] Certain Roman Catholic philosophers and theologians of the 19th century attempted such a proof. However, their position, known as "ontologism," was condemned by the Catholic Church in 1861. See *Denzinger* #1659, which condemns the following proposition: "an immediate knowledge of God, which is at least habitual, is so essential to the human intellect that without that knowledge it can know nothing. It is the light of the intellect itself." Also rejected is the position held by some of the ontologists that the idea of God is elicited spontaneously and naturally within every act of knowing any thing. These expressions might lead one to think of the enormously influential 20th century theologian Karl Rahner. Rahner, however, carefully avoids the propositional assertions involved in these errors in the theoretical construction of his epistemology by means of his novel concept of the *Vorgriff* (literally "pre-grasp"). Rahner will maintain that the *apriori* "pre-grasp" of the existence of the Infinite Mystery that habitually constitutes the intellect and is actualized in every act of knowledge is not an *idea*, or any kind of "thematic" knowledge. Indeed, in his attempt to overcome the Kantian critique of objective knowledge, Rahner creates a special realm within the human intellect itself, which he identifies with the Kantian tinged term "transcendental," but which—like many other 20th century Catholic "critical realists"—he insists pertains not simply to the structural presuppositions by which the mind carries out its thinking process, but rather to the structures inherent in the mind which constitute conditions of possibility that underlie the mind's *actual knowledge* of reality. Rahner's *vorgriff* of the transcendent Mystery, therefore, is neither a habitual nor actual knowledge, nor can it simply be identified with the light of the agent intellect; rather it is *prior* to all of this as structural condition of possibility, or—as Rahner is fond of saying—*horizon*. What he means by this novel terminology is not, in the opinion of this author, particularly clear. There are some who are convinced that the terminology, upon sufficient examination, will result in the conclusion that the difference between Rahner's position and that of the ontologists is merely notional. Nevertheless, because of its peculiar epistemological context and presuppositions, and well as its complex articulation, it is difficult to simply assert that Rahner's theoretical position is the same as ontologism. Whether or not it ultimately succeeds in avoiding the existential *dangers* regarding the human approach to God that in part

Perhaps placing the question in a broader anthropological context might provide a clue. Let us ask: is there any naturally implanted "religious awareness" that "comes with" the fundamental structure of the human soul? St. Thomas, in fact, says that there is a *kind* of natural knowledge of God innate to human beings. It is not, however, an *innate idea*, and is not sufficient of itself for any kind of proof. He calls it a "general and confused" knowledge:

> To know that God exists in a general and confused way is implanted in us by nature, inasmuch as God is man's beatitude. For man naturally desires happiness, and what is naturally desired by man must be naturally known to him. This, however, is not to know absolutely that God exists; just as to know that someone is approaching is not the same as to know that Peter is approaching.[23]

This is a very interesting text. What it implies is that while the *knowledge* of God's existence is not innate to man, there is an awareness and orientation innate to man for a beatitute that, *in fact*, corresponds only to the reality of God, even though man does not know this fact *a-priori*.

Man, by his very nature, by the very structure of his spiritual personality, is oriented toward a "beatitude," an ultimate reality which explains everything else, which

---

motivated the Catholic Church's condemnation of ontologism is another question.

[23] *Summa Theologiae* I, q. 2, a. 1.

perfects everything and perfects himself, an ultimate reality which his life is "for". To live "for" something ultimate and final, complete and perfect, something that orders and explains everything else and gives purpose and significance to everything else, an ultimate reality that is inexhaustible and that promises to make man permanently happy: man can no more do without this than he can do without eating and drinking (in fact men will give up eating and drinking before they will abandon their ultimate hope). We will discuss this more when we speak about God as man's "final end". We could also call this factor within man's life his inescapable orientation toward *fulfillment*. A man can deny God's existence, but his heart cannot fail to live for something that he judges (or wills) to be ultimate (i.e. to be the ultimate *good*, the object that will finally fulfill him). This is why the *real choice* is not between God and atheism but between God and idols. When man abandons God he necessarily creates idols (whether they be cultic idols [paganism] or secular ideological idols [Marxism, humanism, consumerism, etc.]).

Much of modern philosophy since the 19th century has tried to assert that the meaning of the word "God" is more or less identified with the innate force of the human quest for ultimate meaning and purpose. Having turned man in upon himself, modern philosophy abandoned the possibility of proving God's existence from the external world. Nevertheless, man—looking into himself—could not escape this need for ultimate fulfillment within him. And, as St. Thomas already pointed out, the tendency of man's nature toward its ultimate end does constitute a kind of "general and confused" knowledge of God. However, this obscure awareness becomes an explicit affirmation, a certainty, a propositional judgment (even on the level of common sense) only through man's encounter with created beings in the world that—in pointing to their Source—also point toward man's Origin and his final End.

Cut off from the world, however, the intellect of the modern philosopher has only this inner sense of the Absolute. He tries to claim that this inner sense is the sole *source* of the notion of God and the judgment that He exists. Thus God is said to be a necessary postulate of the mind; i.e. the assertion is made that—even though we cannot know God's existence by the reasoning from things in the world—we must *posit* it as the term of the subjective experience of human searching, human incompleteness, or the radical inner experience of a feeling of piety toward the Absolute. In such a manner, the famous Protestant philosopher of religion Friedrich Schleiermacher tried in the beginning of the 19th century to re-establish the credibility of Christianity in the face of Enlightenment skepticism.[24] His attempt seemed attractive to some (and indeed gave birth to a whole movement of religious thought which has come to be known as "liberal Protestantism") perhaps because—as St. Thomas points out—man's natural inclination and desire for beatitute is an *indicator* that points to God. But in and of itself it is an obscure indicator. It is easily manipulated and directed toward objects other than the true God, precisely because it does not present God clearly to the mind as an object.[25] Given the position of

---

[24] Schleiermacher's *On Religion: Speeches to its Cultured Despisers* first appeared in print in 1799.

[25] Thus St. Thomas continues in the reply to the first objection in ST I, q. 2, a. 1: "many there are who imagine that man's perfect good which is

An Essay in the Philosophy of Religion

Schleiermacher and others like him in the first part of the 19th century, it is not surprising that someone eventually came along who was bold enough to take things one step further and thus recast the entire issue. Such a man was the German philosopher Ludwig Feuerbach, who claimed (not unreasonably, given the above premises) that "God" is an idea invented by man as a projection of his own aspirations to be perfectly powerful, free, and happy; indeed, for man *himself* to be lord and master of the universe.[26] From this perspective, it was a small step to advocate replacing the idea of God with the idea of *man*. Indeed, why not acknowledge that the idea of God is a poor and primitive substitute for—indeed an evasion of—the task of man to affirm himself to an unlimited degree. In the contemporary world, it is not only the Marxists of unhappy memory who have attempted to carry out this task; a wide variety of secularist ideologues have attempted to carry out the project of absolute, autonomous human progress in various ways.

---

happiness, consists in riches, and others in pleasures, and others in something else."

[26] Feuerbach's *The Essence of Christianity* (1841) began a new epoch in the philosophy of religion. For the first time, a radical atheism could be viewed not only as rationally defensible, but as *necessary* for human progress. It was not long before the genius of Karl Marx would combine Feuerbach's theory with Hegelian dialectic, supposedly "scientific" materialism, and a mystical evolutionary humanism to produce the powerful system of thought that was to become so influential and so destructive in the twentieth century. Feuerbach's own theories on religion show a marked influence of the Protestant theology he learned as a divinity student. Of particular interest is his essay *The Essence of Faith According to Luther* (1844), in which he seeks the connection between his own anthropological reduction of Christianity and the aspirations inherent in the expressions of the religious genius who founded the Protestant reformation.

Even from a sociological point of view, however, one would expect more people to realize that autonomous man's project of self-divinization has had its day. What have been its obvious fruits? It has produced two world wars in the most murderous century in human history, a political regime that everyone now admits was the most cruel and tyrannical ever conceived by man, and it is well on its way to bringing about the moral, social, and cultural disintegration of the Western world. As Pascal once noted, man is a rather absurd god.

It is time for the 21st century to admit at least that the word "God," if it has meant anything at all in the venerable speech of countless generations of human beings, must mean something *other* than the psychologically repressed desire to unfold without rule or measure the occult potentialities of man or to express the contradictory and all too often violent hungers of an alienated human spirit adrift in an impersonal universe.

[3] Excursus on St. Anselm's Argument

There is another form of argument for the existence of God which at least *appears* to be an apriori argument; this is the so called "ontological argument" generally identified with St. Anselm, although it has taken various forms in the history of philosophy. The various types of ontological arguments attempt to proceed from an *idea* of God to the necessity of his existence.

St. Anselm's own version of the argument, however, has a peculiar and complex character that makes it particularly difficult to understand. What Anselm appears to be saying,

An Essay in the Philosophy of Religion

in the final analysis, amounts to something like this: human beings encounter in some *direct* fashion, from out of their experience of created things, an intellectual perception of the Divine Perfection that is *as such* self-verifying. One need only attain to the idea of the Divine Perfection, through a relatively simple reasoning process, in order to grasp—*by means of the very idea itself*—that God must exist.[27]

St. Thomas in fact points out that the existence of God is "self-evident" *in itself*. For anyone who encounters the essence of God as an object, it is impossible to deny the existence of God—because existence is proper to the essence of God: He is His existence. To see Him is to "see" subsistent existing. But, as St. Thomas also points out, we don't see the essence of God in this life. So Thomas concludes that God's existence is not self-evident *to us*. We do not encounter Him directly as an object of our experience. Rather what we encounter are His effects, and so we must proceed a-posteriori to conclude to His existence; we must start with what we know "first"—contingent beings.[28]

St. Anselm's ontological argument, however, is stated in several different ways in the course of the *Proslogion*. The most well-known version goes like this: "To think about the greatest conceivable being you have to think of it as actually existing, because if you thought about the greatest conceivable being as non-existing, then it would be possible to think of one more being still greater, the greatest conceivable being with existence too. So the understanding

---

[27] See his *Proslogion*, chs. 2-3.
[28] ST I, q. 2, a. 1.

of a being greater than which nothing can be conceived includes its real existence." This is the clever piece of conceptual analysis that has generated so much debate over the centuries. Here St. Anselm seems to be saying that you can move from the *concept* of a being greater than which nothing can be conceived to the *judgment* that this being really exists. He begins his argument with a concept and says that the affirmation of real existence is included in this concept. It is worth noting here that St. Anselm is right: existence is a perfection, and the all-perfect being would have to possess the perfection of existence. This, however, proves only the conceptual coherence of the idea of God; we don't have the means of moving from the conceptual coherence of the idea to the judgment that such a being actually exists (many atheists, in fact, make use of the idea of a most perfect being not to affirm the existence of God but to define the endpoint of man's constructive activity— the perfect being does not *yet* exist [except in the mind and aspirations and imagination of man], and man must therefore create the most perfect being or rather *become* the most perfect being).

Nevertheless, we are in the habit of reading St. Anselm entirely through the lens of modern philosophical categories. We must remember, however, that Anselm was not a modern idealist. Rather, he was a classical realist of the Augustinian tradition, which means that his understanding of the relationship between the mind and objective reality was much more complex than modern idealism. Therefore we should not be surprised that the ontological argument takes an interesting turn in the response to Gaunilon. In treating Gaunilon's objections, St. Anselm moves effortlessly and without notice into the realm of a-posteriori argumentation. For example, when Gaunilon asks, "where do I get this idea in the first place of

An Essay in the Philosophy of Religion

a being greater than which nothing can be conceived?," St. Anselm refers without the slightest hesitation to *the degrees of perfections in things*, that lead the intellect to the notion of a highest possible perfection.[29] Here the "idea" of a being greater than which nothing can be conceived is clearly not innate to the mind, nor is it an immediate object of human perception that arises "prior" to the knowledge of things; rather it is a concept arrived at through a-posteriori reasoning from the observable perfections in things. Perhaps in this sense, "conceiving" shows itself to be not the modern abstract process of combining notions in the mind, but the eminently Augustinian intellectual process of reasoning from created beings to the source that they signify *under the action of Divine illumination*. And so, "I see this being existing with this degree of perfection, and then I see that being existing with a greater degree of perfection, and I am enlightened by the Divine light to move from these particulars to the universal, from the various images to their archtype. I therefore come to the conclusion that there must be some definitive instance of perfection, and it can be said—in the Augustinian sense—that my mind has been 'led' to this notion of an incomparably highest perfection from the perfections in things. Such Perfection would be the Total Perfection, of which all perfections in created realities are images. But it would be senseless to claim that this highest perfection ("Perfection" in the proper sense) does not exist when the lower perfections (which are signs leading me to it) *do exist*." In this sense, it seems that St. Anselm's argument is distinct from the efforts of modern subjectivism. Rather, the original version of the "ontological argument" involves a kind of analysis of "Absolute Perfection" within an Augustinian framework. Thus, it requires at least in some sense an 'a-posteriori' point of departure from the

---

[29] *Reply to Gaunilo*, ch. 8. St. Anselm, in fact, concludes this chapter with the quotation from Romans 1:20.

experience of things in the world. In this respect, it is not entirely unlike the *fourth* way of Aquinas.[30]

---

[30] These few pages clearly cannot even begin to do justice to the subtleties involved in dealing with St. Anselm. They are merely suggestive of reasons why we might want to regard Anselm as someone more than "the guy who tries to argue for God's existence in a way that anyone can see doesn't work." The resemblance in certain respects between Anselm's argument and the fourth way of St. Thomas Aquinas also illustrates the contextual continuity and common assumptions that link St. Thomas's thought to his predecessors and his contemporaries (a link that is often insufficiently stressed). Even given such an interpretation of Anselm's argument, however, the fourth way of St. Thomas Aquinas strikes us as a more adequate argument because it is rooted in a more refined metaphysics and epistemology. Anselm never really hits upon the key to the argument from perfection; namely, that gradations of perfection have to do with the possession of increased levels of *being*, which must be accounted for by a *cause*. On the whole, it was one of the great achievements of Aquinas to bring the Augustinian notions of participation and exemplarism into a synthesis with the Aristotelian understanding of causality. Moreover, preThomistic Christian philosophy and theology in the Middle Ages (once again, largely using the great but sometimes unclarified insights of Augustine) did not clearly distinguish the two aspects of mental activity: apprehension and judgment. They identified reasoning as the work of human intelligence perceiving reality under specific acts of illumination from God. For this reason too it is difficult in the Augustinian tradition to discern where philosophical reasoning ends and theological reasoning (or indeed infused contemplative wisdom) begins. [Thus St. Bonaventure can make his famous ardent and dramatic statement—true indeed for the mystic (and thus ultimately *for man*) but rather beguiling for philosophy in its plodding reasoning process founded on the things of nature: *"The Cross of Christ—that is my only metaphysics!"*] It was Aquinas once again who would brilliantly bring about the synthesis of Augustinian illuminationism and the Aristotelian understanding of the *agent intellect*. This insight of Aquinas on this matter has not been sufficiently appreciated: he identified the agent intellect of Aristotle as a created participation of each human intellect in the Divine Light, which meant that the intellect itself could *illumine*, through the process of abstraction, as a proper secondary cause under the primary causality of God. Thus the human intellect, in its being and in its activity, truly reflects the image of God.

IV. THE PERSONALISTIC APPROACH

[1] Can one argue for the existence of God based on factors which man perceives within himself?

It should be clear from what we have considered that none of man's efforts to rely *exclusively* on an introspective analysis of himself—his own ideas, needs, desires—while holding in suspension his original experience of lived contact and engagement with the realities of the world will lead him to God. Indeed all of these efforts, however well intentioned, impoverish man's sense of the concrete significance of God in his life. They abandon the realm of real things to agnosticism, and thus in the end lead to the secularization of life, because it is this world of real things that energizes man's reason and awakens his freedom. Man's taste for life begins by his being immersed within reality, and if there is no connection between this "taste" and God, then it is not likely that a vigorous and healthy human person is going to take God seriously.

At this point, it is worthwhile to digress briefly on the meaning of a much misused word in our culture: *experience*. What exactly do we mean by "experience" and what is the value of arguing from it? Everybody today talks about experience, and it seems in popular language to be almost a synonym for subjectivism, at least when the experiences have to do with aspects of life that transcend the empirical order. Let us therefore sharply distinguish two diverse senses in which this word is used; thus we will be able to see that the more common usage of today is really based on an improper sense of the word. In fact, I would say that the problem in our society today is not that we rely too much on experience, but the *opposite*—we largely ignore real experience in favor of ideological constructions.

The improper sense of experience tends to identify it as a kind of personal hermeneutical principle by which the human being actively interprets the raw material of the external world so as to engage life in some sort of consistent way. When most people talk about "experience," when they say "my experience" and "your experience," what they really mean is *my personal interpretation*, my intellectually and emotionally subjective processing of facts and circumstances and external stimuli. So experience is used to refer to the subjective slant that we put on everything by virtue of our expectations, sentiments, preconceptions, sociocultural background, temperament, wits, and our choice of what we want to emphasize and what we want to ignore. No wonder "experience" is the great excuse for intellectual and moral relativism—everyone's experience, in this sense, is diverse.

Now why does everyone tend to think of experience in terms of "my personal interpretation of things"? It is rooted in the epistemological outlook that dominates our culture. If the meaning of everything that cannot be empirically measured must take its origin from the construction of the mind, if the starting point for knowledge (at least in these areas) is myself instead of real things, then the starting point for experience is also myself, my subjective perceptions as interpreted and organized by me, and not the reality of things and the objective "truths" which these realities signify.

What is the proper and original sense of the term "experience"? *Experience has to do with the way in which reality impresses itself upon me, and the way that my faculties respond to reality.* Experience has to do with the way that the truth of things communicates itself to me and manifests itself within the various levels of my awareness. Differences in people's experiences are secondary and accidental; fundamentally the structure of human experience is the same for everyone. There is an *objective character* to the way that my sensibility, imagination, intellect, and will are actualized by their contact with real things in the ordinary carrying out of human life. Experience, in its immediate sense, is generated by my perceiving things, thinking about things and dealing with them and reacting to them and responding to them according to their objective characteristics and my objective cognitive structures. But, by a reflexive act, I can "look" at my experience, I can look at the way I engage beings outside of myself and make that the object of my explicit reflection. This means, however, looking at my "experience of things" objectively, how it actually is, not how I wish it were, how I think it ought to be, what I'd like to ignore or forget. Considering the way I *really* experience things (and distinguishing that from the wishful thinking and interpretation that I tend to impose upon things) is actually a very intellectually rigorous and demanding activity.

Real experience has an objective character, and it is necessary to recall people to this objective way that humans sense things, know things, hope for things, fear things, choose things. This genuine attention to human experience is the self-reflexive aspect of *realism*. Just as the objective character of things outside the mind—which everyone acknowledges with their common sense—must be the basis for rational reflection upon the world, so also the objective character of the human experience of reality—which, once again, no sane person doubts in ordinary life—must be the basis for rational reflection on *man*. Things act according to their nature. Things act according to the way they are: "*agere sequitur esse*," according to expression of the perennial philosophy. The human being acts according to his nature, and so an objective look at how I act (rather than a subjective self-interpretation, the personal ideology that everyone today invokes in the name of "their own experience") will reveal *what I am*.

Remember, as long as we affirm realism, we can examine human experience, confident that experience has an objective character. And we can say to a person in today's culture: "Pay attention to your own experience. But *really* pay attention to it. Don't censure anything that doesn't fit your preconceived scheme, don't explain away factors that contradict your idea about what a human being is. (So for example, don't start out by *defining* human being as solely material, with the result that you are forced to give a dishonest reductive interpretation to all the *spiritual experiences* that characterize human life.) Look at all of human experience and *do justice to all its factors*.[31]

With this in mind, we can see that there is some value to approaches to God that take a more *psychological* road, that examine man's inner life and find therein forceful and

---

[31] For a particularly penetrating analysis of the proper understanding of experience and its necessity for realism, see Luigi Giussani, *The Religious Sense*, chs. 1-3.

persuasive evidence for God. What must be remembered, however, is that their persuasive power presupposes (at least implicitly) some kind of conviction "already" arising out of man's experience of the world. This is because only *after* man encounters and experiences reality does he discover "himself." His self emerges into action in his knowing and loving other persons and other things. In reflecting upon this action, man discovers the distinctive sign of his own mysterious personality. Only in this way can he truly analyze his own "personal" experience. He can, indeed, discover the personal, subjective resonance of the ontological evidence for the existence of God within his own inner psychological experience as a *personal being*. We might say that what can be *known* naturally about God's existence from the world can be confirmed *through an examination of human consciousness*, i.e., when a person looks at himself, and examines himself as a kind of being who knows and loves realities outside of himself.[32] Here we seek to identify the *personalistic* dimension of the natural approach to God, which is something entirely different from the attempt to reach God by leaping beyond the walls of a self-enclosed subjectivity.

This kind of personal psychological approach to God is firmly rooted in the Christian tradition; and although its classic form resembles the modern subjectivist arguments in some respects, it differs from them in a crucial respect, as we shall see. It is the line generally followed in the great philosophico-theological traditions that flow from

---

[32] Here we may appear to be entering into the domain often referred to as "phenomenology." Hopefully, however, it has been made clear that any phenomenological analysis we engage in presupposes and is founded upon a realist epistemology.

Augustine and the Greek Fathers, and in the meditative theology of the early medieval monastic tradition that reaches its pinnacle in St. Bernard. This approach, indeed, is solid enough that it is capable of being formulated by the high scholastics, and St. Thomas himself is no stranger to it. It is, simply, the affirmation of the existence of God that follows from the "natural desire" man experiences for the Infinite Good.

The first ten books of St. Augustine's *Confessions* might be considered an extensive existential presentation of this way of discovering the Mystery of God. Immanentist arguments for God often appeal to the authority of St. Augustine's experience and his famous statement: "You have made us for Yourself, O Lord, and our hearts are restless until they rest in You." However, the key problem for this aspect of modern philosophy of religion—as we have already noted—is that it relies *exclusively* on man's subjective experience of a need for the Infinite, an experience drawn entirely from an examination of the inner landscape of a human consciousness cut off from the created things of the world. It then claims that the analysis of this need, perceived by the subject through a direct inner experience essentially disconnected from any certitudes about the external world, is the *only* way that human beings can be certain of God's existence.

We have also noted St. Thomas's observation that man does have a kind of implicit "sense" of God "built into his subjectivity" (if you will) insofar as he naturally desires happiness, *beatitude*, the absolute, all-fulfilling Good. Nevertheless, man cannot know what this Good is (apart from revelation) unless he "works it out" (so to speak) by dealing with the goods that he encounters in the world and allowing them to *lead* him to some understanding of the proper existence of a transcendent and creative Good.

Here, however, is where the classical "existential" approach to God differs from modern subjectivist approaches. It does not carry out a purely immanent analysis of man's innate desire for beatitude. Rather it considers this desire *in the light of man's experience of finite things which do not satisfy it.* It also relies on a crucial bit of objective reasoning drawn from our observance of the inherent significance of "natural desires" as we encounter them in the world of things.

In logical terms, the argument could be articulated as follows: (1) Man has a natural desire for unlimited Truth, Goodness, and Beauty; (2) Nothing in the finite universe can satisfy this desire; (3) Therefore, if there is no real object that corresponds to man's ultimate desire, then his ultimate desire is in vain; (4) But a desire of nature is never in vain; (5) Therefore man's ultimate desire must have an infinite object corresponding to it.[33]

Of course, some objections to this argument immediately spring to mind. Does man really have a natural desire for unlimited Truth, Goodness, and Beauty? Although we can indeed say that such a desire is at the origin and is the ultimate motivation for human action, the desire itself is not clear at this first level of experience, and—as we have

---

[33] A nice, concise presentation of the argument from desire is presented in a book that deserves to be recommended overall for both its intelligence and its accessibility to the general reader: I am referring to *Handbook of Christian Apologetics* by Peter Kreeft and Ronald K. Tacelli (Downers Grove, Illinois: InterVarsity Press, 1994). The argument is presented on pp. 78-81. The book in general would be useful for anyone interested in a synthetic and logical treatment of various controversial issues in theism and Christianity.

The Created Person and the Mystery of God

already noted—St. Thomas was well aware of the ease with which the human intellect could misunderstand the meaning of the ultimate desire and identify it with a need for some merely finite good. It is only through an analysis of human action—human engagement of finite things in the world—that this desire manifests its deep rootedness in the person and its unlimited scope.

It also does not seem certain, at least at the beginning, that human desire does not have a finite satisfaction. In his treatise *On the Love of God*, St. Bernard proposes the pursuit of and dissatisfaction with various finite goods as a kind of "thought experiment," and even considers the hypothesis of attaining possession of all the finite goods in the universe (which, he points out in his unflappable realism, man would not have the time to achieve). This leads him to conclude, it would seem inductively, that no created thing can completely satisfy the heart of man.[34] St. Augustine, by constrast, had no need for a hypothetical consideration of the matter as he had ample personal experience of the disappointments and limitations of created goods pursued solely for themselves. One could of course object that the logical move from individual experiences to a universal conclusion is merely a dialectical argument (although it would be a strange objection if it were raised within the intellectual climate of today which places such great emphasis on the theoretical value of the *hypothesis* and its experimental verification). Here, however, we are dealing with a valid inference of the practical order; as St. Bernard indicates, the human search for happiness possesses such urgency that man can scarcely afford the

---

[34] See his *Treatise on the Love of God*, ch. 7.

luxury of toying endlessly with possibilities once the invariable pattern of man's constant desire for "more" than what he presently possesses has been sufficiently observed.[35]

The other major objection would challenge the premise that a desire of nature is never in vain. Why not? It would seem that lots of our desires are in vain. My desire to marry a particular person, to be rich, to have a steak dinner, etc—all of these desire may end in frustration. Perhaps then it is true—as certain twentieth century writers like Bertrand Russell have expressed with such an eloquent yet strange blend of stoicism, desperation, and utopian idealism—that man is a paradoxical spark in the midst of nothingness, destined to be extinguished yet attaining a kind of grandeur nonetheless by his ardent aspiration for goodness, flaming out like the brief splendor of fireworks in the night sky; man accepts with courage and with a noble sadness that the Good does not exist, but that he must still enact his small good deeds while he can, before he and his deeds are swallowed by the void. We admire those who accept misfortune and frustration of their desires with dignity and go on being gracious. Perhaps this is the ideal of the whole of man's existence.[36]

Such reflections are a kind of poetic expression of the soul of twentieth century man, with his desperate need to

---

[35] "If you would lay hold upon that which, once grasped, leaves no more to be desired—what is the necessity of putting the rest to the test? You run along bypaths and you will die long before you attain the object of your desires along this circuitous route" (*On the Love of God*, ch. 7).

[36] See, for an example of this kind of rhetoric, Bertrand Russell, "A Free Man's Worship," in *Mysticism and Logic and Other Essays* (London: Allen and Unwin, 1951), pp. 46-47.

affirm meaning even though he has ruled out, apriori, the possibility of meaning. Otherwise, however, they make no sense. Moreover, our age has witnessed how the small good deeds of godless man quickly degenerate into veiled or open violence. One recalls Walker Percy's incisive observation regarding the "niceness" of the secular world: "tenderness leads to the gas chamber."

In any case, however, it is worth noting that the objection is ill conceived from the very beginning. It does not deal fairly with *desires of nature*, but instead confuses them with desires elicited by the particular circumstances that are encountered, that draw out and specify more fundamental needs rooted in nature. All of the desires that we perceive as built into nature have objects that correspond to them, whether they be hunger, thirst, sexual desire, or the need for love. None of these desires are in vain; that is, none of them lack an essential object that corresponds to them, even though a particular attempt to satisfy one of these desires may fail to achieve the particular object it is aiming at. The preference of my appetite on a particular evening may not attain its desired object, a steak dinner. Nevertheless, the desire of my bodily nature—hunger—does have an object corresponding to it—food. There are also realities that essentially frustrate it, such as poison. Similar examples abound for any natural desire we can think of.

Are we then to say that every desire of nature has an object except the most fundamental desire, the desire that underlies every other human desire, the desire for Truth and Love without limit? Such an assertion empties the universe of purpose; indeed it renders the universe a cruel joke. It makes no sense even to continue talking. Yet this universe in which God is absent is full of talking. From whence, then, comes this desire to say something meaningful, to do what is "good?" From whence comes this implacable hope to be happy? It makes sense only if the ultimate Good, the ultimate Perfection of all life, really exists.

[2] Excursus: More Psychological Approaches to God

[a] Gabriel Marcel's Argument from Fidelity

It has been noted—by Nietzsche, interestingly enough—that man is the only being in nature who is capable of making a promise. Gabriel Marcel—the 20th century Christian existentialist philosopher—thinks that the absolute character of a promise is an indicator of God's existence.[37]

Human beings are capable of this amazing gesture: the promise of unconditional fidelity. "I will always love you, I will always be true to you." Such a promise is intended as a total and irrevocable gift of the self; it is not honest if it is hedged with any conditions or limitations whatsover. Man makes such promises of total fidelity with a basic confidence that the commitment is genuine, and that the "forever" contained within it is a real possibility. But

---

[37] For a synthesis of this argument, I am indebted to the excellent work of Aidan Nichols, O.P., *A Grammar of Consent* (Notre Dame: University of Notre Dame Press, 1991), pp. 153-163. Nichols indicates the importance of the first essay in Marcel's book *Homo Viator* [trans. Emma Crawford (New York: Harper and Row)] entitled "Sketch of A Phenomenology and a Metaphysic of Hope" (pp. 29-67). I would also refer the reader to another important work of Marcel entitled *Creative Fidelity*, which is in an English translation by Robert Rosthal (New York: Farrar, Straus, and Giroux, 1964). See pp. 157-173, especially p. 167.

what—Marcel asks—is the foundation for my confidence? Is it within myself? Are my personal resoluteness and integrity impeccable? Is it not, rather, always within me to betray, to deceive, to fall short, to fail in love? Is it in the other person? But that person is of the same limited nature as I! Is it in the circumstances? The circumstances of every human relationship are fragile and threatened by the possibility of separation and death. Therefore, the human promise of unconditional fidelity to another is either foolish, or a lie, or it is grounded in Something that cannot fail—a Being absolutely faithful who can guarantee and render secure my own fidelity.

Thus we note something very interesting: the human promise reaches the fullness of its unconditional stature by taking the form of a *vow* (which we see manifested in different ways in various religions). Man has—historically—grounded and guaranteed his promises by invoking the Divine. On the other hand, to the degree that a society loses its sense of God, fidelity between human persons is compromised, and relationships are shipwrecked on the rocks of human limitations.

[b] Some Reflections on the Mystery of Childhood

One of the more powerful ways in which human beings, upon reflection, can encounter the mystery of God at the heart of (seemingly) ordinary experience is through a careful analysis of what is involved in the relationship between parents and children.

When you conceive and have a child and start raising him, you see very clearly that this new little entity is in some sense the effect of the combined causal activity of you and your spouse. He is flesh of your flesh; he has both physical and temperamental characteristics that clearly come from you, and that you observe in countless ways right from the start of his life in the world.

At the same time, it is also clear almost from the start—and it becomes clearer and clearer as time goes on—that there is another dimension to this little being, that what is deepest and most central to him is something that *did not come from you*; he has his own personhood, his own incommunicable identity which blossoms forth as he grows into his own personal capacity to know you and love you freely—to enrich you with something *from himself*, something that you did not "already" possess and that you did not *cause* in him.

It is clear that you and your spouse are not responsible for—you are not the proper and primary efficient causes of—*who he is*. You did not cause (and you do not possess within yourselves) that which makes him to be the wonderful, unique, mysterious, and precious person that he is. There must have been some Greater Cause involved.

Or consider from another point of view the astounding disproportion between the sexual act, in all of its fragility and contingency, and the *person* who is conceived consequent upon this act. Even when the sexual act is performed according to the design of God—prayerfully, as an interpersonal act, as an expression of spousal love and openness to new life—it remains something quite limited and circumstantial, something which may not take place because of a telephone call or a headache. And then, even if it does take place, there are millions of possible genetic combinations and only one of them—perhaps—gets realized. Here are the causal factors that we observe in the process. And what is the effect? A person, unique,

The Created Person and the Mystery of God

unrepeatable, individual, possessed of a greater dignity than the whole material universe, capable of knowledge and self-awareness, capable of heroism, capable of amazing the world by expressions of beauty, capable of undying love.

Clearly, the causes we observe do not provide a sufficient explanation for the effect that results. There must be some other Cause involved in the coming-into-being of a child, a Cause that can account for the fact that a new and different human person now exists.[38] And in order to bestow spiritual personhood, this Cause must be the very Source of Personality and therefore eminently Personal Himself.

It is not surprising, therefore, that human cultures have always been inclined to attach a religious significance to the conception and birth of a child and the familial environment in which a child is educated. A reflection on the fruit of spousal love manifests in a particularly evident way its *awesome* character. Indeed "a child is a gift from God," as the human heart almost spontaneously affirms in the measure in which it is not entirely distorted and suffocated by the culture of death. Even today, in spite of the massive effort to regard human "reproduction" as just another task to be managed and dominated by technological power, a little child—encountered on the sidewalk or in a store riding in a shopping cart—evokes wonder and joy in those who see him. In his very newness he is a special sign of the

---

[38] These observations are not foreign to the ancient Christian tradition. One can find in St. Gregory of Nyssa (4th century) a remarkably similiar reflection: Gregory argues forcefully that there must be the intervention of Divine power in the act of human procreation on account of the disproportion between the visible antecedent cause and its effect. See the *Catechetical Orations*, ch. 33.

An Essay in the Philosophy of Religion

Mystery that is his origin, the Mystery that is the only adequate "reason" that can account for his being there, a new reality in an old world, a new face.

V. MAN: A RELIGIOUS BEING

[1] Philosophical Foundations

As the basis for concluding our reflections in Part I, let us return to the insight of St. Thomas that we examined earlier. We noted that his argument from the *De Ente et Essentia* concludes that there must be a Primary Cause that accounts for the existence of things; that gives to all other things their act of being. As First Cause it is the Origin of all existing which means that it does not receive its act of existing from anywhere else—it possesses "existing" properly as the very definition of what it is. Its essence is "to exist;" it is the subsistent, pure act of "to be." From these considerations, it follows that *our* existence does not come from ourselves; it is a gift from the One who possesses Existence fully because He *is* Existence.

Now here, I would maintain, we have not only a powerful demonstration of God, but also a particularly clear indication of the basic characteristic of *creaturehood*—the total ontological dependence of the creature on God the Creator. The fundamental actualization of every being, and therefore the influx of ontological "energy" that constitutes the difference between "John exists" and "John does not exist" comes directly from God. Moreover the recognition of this dynamic character of existing enables us to have a much richer understanding of what St. Thomas means by "divine conservation." Chapter 65 of the third book of the *Summa Contra Gentiles* is the remarkable text that explains why it is necessary for God to preserve all things in being. Here Thomas draws a direct comparison between the

Divine operation that creates things and the application of physical force to *move* a corporeal object.[39]

To appreciate the import of this text, we must not allow ourselves to be distracted by Thomas's primitive understanding of experimental physics. Rather, we must appreciate the camparison as an illustrative metaphor for the metaphysical truth about God's sustaining causality. We sustaining causality. We must also remember that, in the context of Thomas's thought, *motion* is not understood mechanistically; rather it is regarded as the realization of the potentiality of some being with regard to place. Thus a thing in motion is a thing that is changing with regard to a certain attribute of its being. And such change, because it radically involves the realization of some aspect of reality not previously possessed, must be caused by another.

With these considerations in mind, we may proceed to an appreciation of Thomas's comparison. He observes that, just as continuous application of physical force is necessary for continued motion of an object, so a continual Divine operation is necessary for the continued existence of the creature. Just as the leaves rustle only as long as the wind is blowing through them, so also I *exist* only as long as the Divine creative power is "blowing" through me.

This analysis of the complete ontological dependence of creatures on God's creative causality points to the metaphysical foundation for the *religious* character of existence. Let us consider St. Thomas's understanding of creaturehood as it applies specifically to the human person. "I" am a creature. My existing is totally, utterly dependent on God. My existing *in this moment*, your existing *in this*

---

[39] *Summa Contra Gentiles,* III, 65.

moment, the existing of everything in this moment is totally and completely the effect of God's creative and sustaining causality. Right now, everything is being "energized" in its existence by the application of Divine power. Right now, *I, myself*, in my inscrutable personal mystery, along with my intellect, my will, my affections, my senses, my imagination, my speech—all are vitalized by God, distinguished from nothingness only by God's continual call to being. The implication is clear: "I" belong to God; He possesses me completely, and my existence is entirely His gift. And this belonging, this total dependence, this gift-character of my existence is not just something that defined the original moment when I first came into being. *It defines every moment of my existence.* The God who knit me together in my mother's womb still holds me together in His strong embrace. My existing is the effect of a relationship, a constant relationship, a totally dependent relationship with the One who creates and sustains me. So we see that the religious sense which is at the heart of our obligation to submit our human reason to God, the religiosity that is in any case essential to man's natural life, is not something that is extorted from man by an overbearing Divine Will that simply wants to assert its superiority and dominion by impinging upon the freedom and autonomy of man. Man's natural religious life consists in the gratitude and the wonder and the responsiveness of his intelligence and his freedom to the here-and-now gift of his existence, and to the Giver upon whose presence he is totally dependent. The grateful acknowledgement of the Creator-creature relationship is the eminent exercise of human reason.

[2] The Specific Characteristics of Religion

Man's religiosity is evident both objectively and subjectively—it is revealed by both philosophical analysis and psychological analysis. We can see that *religion*—man's responsibility to worship and serve God—has a profound metaphysical foundation. It is not surprising that man—as a *person* capable of self-awareness—can also discover and indeed deepen his sense of this responsibility from a serious reflection upon his experience of life, of the world, and of himself. Indeed, man's orientation toward God is written into the very core of the structure of his heart.

The human person has a universal energy; he aspires to a life without boundaries, to a full realization, to a limitless awareness and a limitless love. Indeed, the human person—as a being who transcends the material world through knowledge and love—cannot have as his fulfillment material things. Moreover, man's intellect and will seek the true and the good as such, without qualification. Thus they cannot reach the end of their activity as long as there remains any aspect of being that is not yet known and loved. Man is by nature a "seeker," and there is no end to his desire.

This is a point that is most obscured in the culture of today—we live in a world that proposes so many modes of satisfaction for the human being, and yet we are the most unsatisfied people in history. People get what they think they want, but it disappoints them and then they want more. So, just as people need to be "recalled to realism" so that they can grasp the truth about created reality and its Source, so also they need to be recalled to *the true nature of the human heart* so that they can rediscover the nobility, the beauty, and the grandeur of a religious adherence to God. Man must come to realize that, ultimately, only God is adequate to the desire of the human heart.

We have already noted the classic observation of St. Augustine: "Lord, you have made us for Yourself, and our hearts are restless until they rest in You." What do we mean by the "heart"? We could define the heart as the center of the spiritual life of man. Philosophical anthropology distinguishes intellect and will, and yet these powers are not separate in the living man, but operate in a vital unity—indeed they are an extension, an overflowing of the soul's own essential act. The heart, then, is this living unity of man's spiritual inclination toward being. Intellect and will are like the two "chambers" of the heart, working together as a single center that reaches out to embrace reality.

"Our hearts are restless..." What truth is more evident in the world of today than this? "Everybody's got a hungry heart," says a popular song from twenty years ago. Hungry for what? For an absolute, totally fulfilling, infinite *Good*. Our culture has *no answer* for this hunger, and every single human being is walking around with this hunger roaring inside of them—no matter how they might describe themselves, no matter what psychological techniques they may use to push this desire to the edges of their consciousness, *they have it* and it cannot be erased, *not even in hell* (on the contrary, in hell there is no way to distract one's self from the need for God that constitutes one's own heart, and for this reason the eternal "loss" of God is experienced as the greatest possible suffering).

An Essay in the Philosophy of Religion

In light of the metaphysics of creaturehood and the desire for God, let us look at the obligation of religion. Religion is the means by which man orders his life to God. Philosophically, we can recognize that man is obligated to seek God, to orient his whole life toward God, to render to God worship and thanksgiving. Man's existence is a creaturely existence, a *received* existence. And it is a personal existence, capable of knowing and loving its Source. Man's condition of dependence on God ought to be affirmed and embraced as the vital center of man's whole life. Religion is thus the realization of man's creaturely being—it is man fully alive, proceeding from God and returning to God not only in his created act of "to be" but also in the acts of knowing and loving that bring his created existence to perfection.

We have seen that the human being is created by God and for God, so that the significance of his human existence and the task entrusted to his freedom is to affirm God, be aware of God, love God in every moment of the existence God freely gives him. Man is made for an Infinite fulfillment; he is made to order his life—in every detail—in accordance with the God whom he can recognize as the Source of all things; thus we say that man is created as a *religious being*, and that religiosity is the summit of his existence.

Let us examine more closely the various elements that make up the essential structure of man's religious activity:

> [1] *Worship.* God's infinite Being, and His infinite Truth, Goodness, and Beauty are reflected by the profound signification that is to be found in the depths of every being He

has created. Man is led by the mystery of created existence to an acknowledgment of God that is full of wonder and awe. To praise, to adore and glorify the Infinite Mystery who possesses in an ineffable and supereminent way all the loveliness of creation—who is the overflowing Source of every good and every beauty that draws and fascinates the human heart—this is the foundation of worship. And when this praise is consciously and intentionally taken up and offered to God from out of the heart of man, then worship takes on its full stature, and the hymn of glory that all creation sings to God by virtue of all that it is reaches its summit in the personal offering of man. The mysterious sign of the perfection of God imprinted upon each creature and upon the whole of creation finds its voice in human worship, which lifts up the world and consecrates it to God.

[2] *Petition and Thanksgiving.* Man's recognition of his total dependence on God and the freedom and pure love of God's goodness in creating him is expressed and lived personally in the confident asking, full of hope and trust, that man raises to God with regard to all of man's needs. Correspondingly, it also is expressed in a conscious gratitude that man offers for everything, because he recognizes that the truth about every thing is that it is a *gift*. His own existence in every moment is a gift.

Everything in the universe is a gift. Every discovery and every magnanimous movement of the heart is a gift.

[3] *Obedience*. The greatest gift that I receive from God is nothing less than *my very existence*. God gives me a created participation in what is essentially, properly *His*; the gift of existing has God's signature upon it, and it reflects His truth, goodness, and beauty. Thus I must always use this gift in accordance with the loving purposes of the Giver whose own Personal truth is reflected in it. Because it is a *gift*, my existing is truly my own. By God's gift, *I* truly exist and I possess my being as my own. At the same time, this gift remains and always will remain God's, because what in fact constitutes me is *his gesture of love*; it is His uniquely designed and exquisitely crafted gesture of creating love that makes me to be me. For this reason God's will—which is identical to the design of His loving wisdom—is the "law" of my life; it is the truth of my being, because in each moment I am shaped by his mysterious plan. I am myself in each moment because I am called forth by the design of His love for me.

[4] *Love*. It would seem to follow quite naturally that love is the culmination of human religiosity. As the Supreme Good, God is certainly supremely worthy of love, and all of His creatures can be said in some

sense to "love" Him insofar as they pursue the good for which He made them, which is a reflection of His own transcendent Goodness. It is man, however, who becomes aware of the goodness of God as such. Man also grasps, by virtue of the analogy of his own created personhood, that God is Supremely Personal and therefore worthy of interpersonal love in its highest expression. At the same time, however, God is transcendent Personality; He is the Source of all created persons, and is Himself therefore in a very real sense *unapproachable*. It would be presumptuous for man to "claim" God, even out of love. Nevertheless, the religious man loves God "with all his strength," and this love constitutes the "space" within which a word from God might be freely spoken.

Man's responsibility to "practice" religion is shaped by two factors: (1) that man is a created person; and (2) that God is his ultimate end. As we have seen, man—because he is a creature—is totally dependent on God at every moment of his existence. Man's existence *belongs* to God. Moreover, as a *person*, with intelligence and freedom, man is capable of knowing and loving—to the degree that his finite mind permits—the One on whom he depends and to whom he belongs. Man is capable of accepting, concurring, and corresponding in the personal life of his reason and will with the truth of his own creaturely being. A man who does not live his life knowing and loving His Creator is not living in a fully human way; he is blind to the central factor of his own existence. Imagine a child who systematically ignored his parents even as they gave him everything. Everyone would agree that such a child would be nasty, ungrateful, pitiable, and foolish: in a word, *spoiled*. Thus the height of human existence, the height of a reasonable personal existence, is achieved by the religious man, the man whose moral life is crowned by the *virtue of religion*. It is worth noting that St. Thomas considers religion the highest of all the moral virtues, and as a *directive* virtue in that it directs the acts of all the other virtues to the Divine Good.[40]

As noted above, man's responsibility to practice religion also follows from the fact that God is man's ultimate end. The intelligence and freedom of man are made for truth and goodness without limit or qualification. Man does not rest as long as there remains some truth to be known or some good to be possessed and loved. The only "object" that can bring to fulfillment man's knowledge and love is Infinite Truth and Goodness. The frustration of our world today comes from the fact that people seek Infinite Truth and Goodness where it cannot be found. The ironic question of the prophets has never been more relevant: "why do you spend your wages for what is not bread?"

Man cannot be "happy" unless his mind and will are somehow engaged with the Supremely Interesting and Supremely Loveable Object that alone can exhaust their scope. Man therefore must seek to order all the various purposes of his life to this *ultimate* purpose. Once again,

---

[40] See ST II-II, q. 81. It is worth noting that St. Thomas deals with the virtue of religion as a formally human virtue, distinct from the formally supernatural virtues of Faith, Hope, and Charity.

the malaise of our contemporary culture of death is rooted in the fact that so many seek to order their entire lives toward purposes that are essentially incomplete, and therefore ultimately unworthy of the dignity of intelligence and freedom. Ambition, wealth, achievement through work, consolidation of power, vengeance, nationalism, globalism, saving the planet—not to mention sexual pleasure, a life of ease and comfort, indolence, smugness—none of these can serve as an ultimate goal for human life without bringing frustration and bitterness.

We might say that the "posture" of the religious man can be synthetically expressed by the Biblical phrase: "waiting upon the Lord." Religious man seeks the will of God in every circumstance, is open to manifestations or signs of God's will, and is ready to follow these signs wherever they lead because he knows that he belongs to God and that God is his supreme interest in life.

In light of these reflections about the primacy of religion in the life of man, we can see that it is unacceptable to consider religion irrational, unimportant, or peripheral to basic human concerns. The height of human reason, the apex of its realization, is attained when man gives his attention to the Divine and seeks to know and follow God's will. Man without religious interest and awareness is "handicapped" in a manner much more profound than if he lacked eyes or ears; human existence without religion is stunted, suffocated, not worthy of man's personal dignity. And *secularism*—as a social ideology that systematically ignores or marginalizes religion—is an *un*reasonable attack on the personal and social life of man.[41]

[3] Excursus: The Mystery of Evil

There remains the need to mention a particularly difficult psychological roadblock on the path to God which is based on the objective order of things; namely what has been called the "problem" of evil. The existence of evil is a great scandal to many: if God exists and is all powerful and all good, why is there evil in the world? This is a profound question of the existential order; ultimately the answer that satisfies is not so much a theoretical explanation as it is the whole of the Christian event in which God Himself bears all of the evil of the world so as to reveal and communicate Himself as Absolute Love. God's "permission" of evil is, therefore, a mystery that is ultimately resolved in the depths of His love and mercy. There is, however, a metaphysical explanation that is presupposed by what God actually "does" to evil on the Cross. But first let us note that there are basically two options taken by modern theodicy. The contemporary movement known as "process theology" posits a "limited god" who runs the world but is not all-powerful, with the result that evil also exists and will continue to exist until the divinity evolves to an ultimate omnipotence. Classical Enlightenment deism, on the other

---

[41] For further reading on the subject of man as a religious being: one of the finest and most original contemporary treatments of this subject is found in Luigi Giussani's *The Religious Sense*. Chapter 10 in particular is recommended for its lucid and penetrating analysis of how man comes to realizes that he is a created being.

hand, says that God may be all-powerful, but He doesn't run the world, therefore evil exists (such a position is really a preamble to the main point of the rationalist project, which is that man—through the use of his reason—is charged with the grand task of eradicating evil). Whereas Christian metaphysics recognizes that God rules the world, but wills to share His governance with real secondary causes and manifest His omnipotence by bringing good out of their defects. Thus God is all-powerful and all-good, but He wills to create free creatures and therefore permit the *risk* implied by finite freedom; the risk that the free creature will choose something *less than the good.* God's omnipotence is not overcome, however, because He is capable of bringing good (indeed, *greater* good) out of the evil that enters the world through the creaturely misuse of freedom. And although this final point can only be treated adequately in an essay all its own, it is at least worth noting here that, *in fact*, all the evil of our universe has been "used" to glorify God through the greatest good in all of history: the Crucified Heart of Jesus, which embraces and suffers all this evil in order to offer–as the central act of the created universe–His love to the Father and His transforming love and mercy to each and every one of us.

[4] The Possibility of Revelation

We noted at the beginning of this essay that its purpose is to be a preamble to the marvellous truth that in Jesus Christ God has revealed Himself and given Himself to man in an unimaginably intimate way. A discussion of the content and characteristics of this revelation is therefore beyond our scope (although we will address certain aspects of it in Part 4). Everything that we have dealt with here pertains *in principle* to what man should be capable of by virtue of his nature and capacities as a created human person. All that we have discussed would be incumbent upon man even if God had chosen not to reveal Himself, or if He had chosen some other (perhaps lesser) way of engaging in a dialogue with the created person. What we do want to note however is that the possibility of some kind of Divine revelation, some kind of *historical* intervention on the part of God that goes beyond the "givens" of the created order, is profoundly *congenial* to a genuine human religious spirit.

If the summit of man's natural existence is this religious attitude—this seeking to know and to adhere to the will of God in every circumstance—then we can say that man, when he lives the way a man ought to live, would have a profound natural interest in anything that God might wish to *say to him* over and above the witness to God that is given by the created order. Thus we see that man's natural religiosity is *open* to the possibility of some kind of Divine "revelation." If it is true that man lives most fully the dignity of his rational nature by adhering to God's will, then it is clear that were God to take the initiative and *reveal His will to man*, man ought to embrace and follow this revelation. The essentially religous character of human existence thus includes a responsibility to embrace a Divine revelation if God decides to make one. Man's acceptance of such a revelation would be fully in accord with his natural reason and human dignity.

God exists, and man is entirely dependent for his being on God; man's existence is entirely God's gift. Moreover the ultimate purpose of human existence is to know, love, and obey this infinitely generous and loving God who gives to each of us the splendid gift of our being. Therefore, it is reasonable to obey God; indeed we *ought* to follow God's plan for the life He has given us and that He sustains in us. And if He were to reveal this plan—establishing by clear and certain signs that He has spoken to us in history—it would be both morally wrong and intellectually irresponsible not to listen to Him.

Thus we can see that a revelation from God would not contradict man's nature. Rather it would correspond profoundly with man's nature.

There is, moreover, yet another reason—a historical and experiential reason—which gives the question of a possible revelation from God a particular urgency, and which drives the human spirit to *hope* that God might speak a word to man; indeed which drives him to search in so many places for some evidence that a Divine word has been spoken, and a Divine assistance given. It is the fact that man's nature is wounded. Man—in fact—cannot accomplish in an integral fashion the good that his heart desires. Above all when it comes to religion, man is a spectacular failure. He is incapable of the total coherence necessary to live everything for the sake of God; his heart is divided, and he is frustrated. He desires something beyond himself, an expansion of personal life, of knowledge and love, but he is pulled down by distractions and constantly puts his hope in things that are not God and therefore inevitably *disappoint him.*

When he becomes aware of this predicament, man's reason realizes: "I need help!" I need help in dealing with the problem of how to live my life and direct it to its ultimate purpose. "What must I do to be saved?" was the burning question they asked Jesus. And when people ask this question today, they find themselves moving from one scheme to another, from one proposal to another. Why do we live in a society that is saturated with proposed "solutions" to the problem of life? Because the human heart is looking for an *answer*—all you have to do is propose that you have the answer to the riddle of how to live, and you'll get the attention of at least some people no matter how absurd your proposal is. The hunger and thirst of the human heart is so insatiable and so urgent that it will grab hold of anything that presents itself as food for the soul. We are like men dying of thirst in the desert, deceived over and over by mirages that shimmer over dry sand.

The human predicament is this: Man is created for an infinite fulfillment, he is "restless until he rests" in that which is ultimately satisfying—God his Creator. But man does not possess within himself the *means* to attain the fulfillment which he desires; he is frustrated in all the efforts that proceed from his nature and will. His own humanity is somehow inadequate to the central task of his existence, and therefore HE NEEDS HELP from a source outside of himself. At its summit, man's reason, reflecting honestly on his own existence, reaches this conclusion: "I must seek salvation."

Conclusion to Part I

God exists, and man is His creature, a *personal* creature made to know and love God and to seek His will, a creature whose heart transcends the physical universe and longs to adhere to God and to embrace all things for the sake of God; that is, whose heart has been created to live a *religious* existence in its every moment. Man the creature, however, has a mysteriously *divided heart*, which causes him constantly to *fall short* of his exalted destiny; He seeks God among limited, finite things and thus is frustrated. In order to realize the great Divine design for his life, man needs *Divine help*. He must search through the world, through history, to see if the mysterious God has taken some initiative, has offered the help that his wounded heart needs. In the course of this search, man encounters an astonishing claim: the Christian community claims today, as it has for two thousand years, that a particular man in history *embodies fully, unsurpassably*, this Divine help—that a particular man (with flesh and blood) is precisely the "answer," the response of God to man's need, the initiative of God to "save" man; indeed, that He is God Himself come to meet man.

The verification of this claim requires a distinct set of considerations and particular methods that are different than the ones we have employed in this essay. Nevertheless, what we have seen thus far is sufficient to demonstrate that the claim of Christianity is neither extraneous nor marginal to the central questions that constitute man's real life in the world. Whether or not the Christian claim is true is a matter of supreme importance to man; the stand he takes in front of

An Essay in the Philosophy of Religion

Jesus Christ is not merely a matter of abstract convictions or intellectual theories about the workings of the universe; nor is it a mere framework for a series of more or less precisely formulated moral sentiments. Rather the stand that man takes in front of Jesus Christ will determine the way in which he draws each breath of the day. If Christ is truly God's answer to the thirst of my soul, then the only reasonable thing to do is to follow Him.

Part II: Thomistic Roots of a "Fundamental Theology": Studies in the Thought of Jacques Maritain

Introduction

The aim of Part II of this book is to present several studies on the human approach to God and the distinctive metaphysical character of "natural theology" according to the thought of Jacques Maritain. We have cited Maritain numerous times in the essay of Part I not only because he is one of the foremost twentieth century proponents of Thomistic philosophy and epistemological realism, but also because of his acute sensitivity to the impact of modern subjectivist, "anthropocentric"[42] philosophical systems on the realm of culture and its dominant mentality.

Our examination of select technical features of Maritain's highly developed philosophical system will shed further light on the reflections of our essay in Part I. In the first three sections, we will look at how Maritain expresses the Thomistic approach to God in response to the noble but inadequate theories of the great modern philosopher Henri Bergson. Bergson's attempt to circumvent the pure subjectivism of the standard modern philosophical approaches to God still cannot escape the prison of irrationalism; thus Maritain's explanations in response to Bergson have a particular force and clarity that pertains to our affirmation of realism and the inherent capacities of human reason. Maritain distinguishes the precise *analogical* character of our natural knowledge of God, and

---

[42] It is in fact Maritain who coins the phrase "anthropocentric humanism" and the "*anthropocentric* conception of man." See his essay "Integral Humanism and the Crisis of Modern Times," in *Scholasticism and Politics* (Garden City, NY: Doubleday Image Books Edition, 1960 [first edition published 1940]), pp. 12, 17 et alia.

thereby establishes its limits. This allows for a distinct consideration of the supernatural realm of revelation and grace and the possibility of supernatural experiential knowledge that transcends intelligibility (section 4). This "mystical knowledge" has a kind of natural reflection in the experience of beauty, a non-conceptual intellectual perception which—when it attains its transcendental fullness—provides a kind of analogical foretaste of the Beauty who made all beautiful things (section 5). In section 6, we see how Maritain distinguishes between natural and revealed theology, and how the latter is distinguished from philosophy as a whole—both structurally and existentially. Finally, Maritain's clarification of the distinctive character of metaphysics as rooted in the intuition of being manifests the transempirical nature of the human being. Indeed, "common sense" is itself implicitly metaphysical, founded as it is on the primordial intellectual perception of "things" which carries within itself the implicit awareness of "being" as a transcendental. Moreover, Maritain proposes that man is transcendent, ultimately, not simply in his notions but in his very substance. In the final analysis the metaphysical quality of all beings includes the ecstasy by which they achieve their own proper fulfillment. For man this is accomplished in the ecstasy of knowledge and love that aim at the horizon of the Infinite.

[1] Realism and The Mind's Approach To God: Jacques Maritain's Critique of Henri Bergson.

Jacques Maritain's critique of the vitalism of Henri Bergson illustrates the need for the full involvement of human reason in man's natural religious awareness of God. Maritain's understanding of the "natural order"—the manner in which the human being relates to God according to natural, inherent human capacities—is illustrated by the processes of natural human intelligence: the precise manner in which the human intellect grasps the objects proportionate to it by means of the vital activity of its concepts and propositional judgments, and how it then reasons indirectly, by means of analogy, to the existence and attributes of God.

In this study we focus in particular on the principles involved in an epistemological realism in which reason bases its activity on things that really exist in the external world. Thus the approach to God that Maritain develops here is that of natural human reason exercised in its proper rational mode. It should be noted, however, that Maritain himself, in his book *Approaches to God*,[43] has studied the problem of man's coming to a conviction regarding the existence of God in a variety of ways that go beyond the particular analysis he offers here. His study of Bergson, however, provides him with the opportunity to express some fundamental points about the nature of the human intellect that have been neglected or misinterpreted by much

---

43 *Approaches to God*, trans. Peter O'Reilly (New York: Collier, 1962 [original edition 1954]).

of modern philosophy. These points being seen, the *rational* character of man's natural knowledge of God can be clearly perceived and precisely delineated.

Here we are not interested in every specific feature of Maritain's critique of Bergson. Nor do we wish to consider the issue of whether or not Maritain has done justice to Bergson's philosophy. For our purposes here it is sufficient to note the main lines of Maritain's presentation of Bergsonian epistemology, since they form the context for Maritain's own reflections.

According to Maritain, Bergson reduces intelligence to a mechanistic faculty whose concepts and judgments artificially divide up the vital unity of the real. For Bergson, the concept and the reasoning process that composes and divides concepts are artificial constructions of the human intellect which serve the human task of manipulating material reality. When the human mind abstracts and conceptualizes it is, in effect, distancing itself from a lived contact with reality in its fullness in order to fragmentize the real and focus on those "parts" of reality that the human being wishes to make use of for a concrete project. Thus for Bergson the processes of the intellect are nominalistic and functional; conceptualization is the manner in which man "breaks up" the mystery of reality in order to subject it to his domination, to fit it to his plan of action. Bergson then opposes to this "fabricating intellect" another process which is referred to as "intuition". Intuition is the way in which reality is properly attained; it requires man to resist the process of abstraction and conceptualization, indeed to move in the opposite direction in order to plunge into the concrete vitality of the real and experience it "from within". In Bergsonian intuition the human spirit is carried by the impulse of the whole of reality; instead of "freezing" reality in conceptual pictures, it experiences, even if only fleetingly, the dynamism that constitutes all of reality—the genuine character of reality as evolutive, as continual movement and growth, continual bursting forth of the radically new.[44]

Having thus presented Bergson's view of intellect and intuition, Maritain critiques it in a variety of ways. What concerns us here is how Maritain—in reproposing the Thomistic understanding of the *concept* (in opposition to Bergson's theory)—emphasizes the vitality and directness of intellectual knowledge, that the human reasoning process is above all a means of contact with the real, that both apprehension and judgment deserve the name of "intellectual intuition". Maritain is convinced that Bergson's great mistake was to assume that the rationalist intellect of modern philosophy—the intellect that classifies and organizes the impressions of the external world according to the scheme of its own ideas—was the *natural* human intellect, when in fact the rationalist intellect is a reduction of the genuine capacities of the human intellect. Indeed schematic and artificial conceptualization for the purposes of more easily classifying the behavior of aspects of the material universe and more easily manipulating them is characteristic of a certain *type* of reasoning—namely the

---

[44] For my citations I am using the English translation of the revised and augmented edition of *La Philosophie Bergsonienne* (which includes the entire text of the first edition), entitled *Bergsonian Philosophy and Thomism*, trans. Mabelle L. Andison and J. Gordon Andison (New York: Philosophical Library, 1955), hereafter referred to as *BergPhil*. For the key points of Maritain's summary of Bergsonian epistemology, see *BergPhil*, pp. 65-73, 102-116.

reasoning of the empirical sciences and the technical arts. However, this is not the whole (or even the highest part) of intellectual activity. Because Bergson did not realize this, he found it necessary to resort to a nonintellectual intuition in order to establish a *direct* relationship between human perception and things as they really are. Maritain intends to rehabilitate the classical understanding of the role of the concept in knowledge by emphasizing that the concept is not an artifice that stands in between the mind and reality, but rather the means through which the mind contacts the real; indeed it is the mind itself "living" the intelligibility of the thing that the senses have perceived.

One need not require that human spiritual perception abandon itself to an ultimately irrational dynamism of universal evolution in order for there to be true "conformity" between such perception and reality. On the contrary, the intelligibility and inherent purposefulness of things which "formally" determine their being and activity are identified and distinguished by the human intellect. The very principles *by which* things are what they are, by which they act, by which they are dynamic, fecund, vital, pulsing with life and purpose and efficacy—the very principles by which things are what they are, their formal *act*ualizations, are what actualize and inform the spiritual capacity of human intelligence. It is actuality in the mode of *formality* that constitutes a particular thing in its distinctiveness, in its definite characteristics; that constitutes this particular material entity as "a rock" and that particular material entity as "a frog". The very same formalities that constitute material things in their distinctive identities actualize, vitalize, in-form the intellect that knows these things. In knowledge, however, the formal characteristics of things are recognized and delineated precisely as formal; they are "abstracted" from the material entity that they actualize. Thus my intellect knows what a rock is because, when I experience different rocks with my senses, my intellect "abstracts" the intelligible aspect of these rocks, the actuality which makes them *be* rocks, which "forms" them with the essential characteristics of rocks. This form then "impresses" itself upon the spiritual capacity of the intellect; it actualizes the intellect—not in the same way that it actualizes material entities, but according to its own proper character *as a formal principle of those material entities*, that is, as a "universal" intrinsically integrated complexus of formal characteristics. The intellect thus actualized, thus in-formed, *ex*-presses this trans-material, universal, formal principle in a *concept* ("rock") "in which the intellect perceives the object." Conceiving is "a simple, irreducible, active, spontaneous perception that may well be called intuitive for it truly puts us in communication with the real."[45]

Maritain's account of conceptualization repeats the classical Thomistic analysis of "simple apprehension"—the first act of the mind that precedes the process of reasoning and the act of judgment. However, in his efforts to

---

[45] *BergPhil*, p. 104. Maritain further develops and elucidates the Thomistic theory of the concept in many places, most notably in his great work *The Degrees of Knowledge*, where he further emphasizes the importance of the concept as a "formal sign," that is, a sign whose essence it is to signify, which first "makes [something] known, before being itself a known object." See *The Degrees of Knowledge*, trans. Gerald B. Phelan, fourth edition (New York: Charles Scribner's Sons, 1959 [first edition, 1932]), pp 119-128. (Hereafter referred to as *Degrees*.) See also Appendix I of the fourth edition, pp. 387-417, which includes extensive presentation and commentary on texts from Aquinas.

overcome the misrepresentation of the concept as a nominalistic classification that distances the mind from reality, Maritain presents the Thomistic understanding of "concept" with particular nuances and emphases—he stresses that concepts are not mental pictures inside the head, indeed that concepts are not *what* we know but rather the means *by which* we know reality. Indeed, Maritain expresses this last point in a unique manner when he identifies the concept as an "intellectual intuition" or a "simple perception".

The concept is the means by which the intellect "sees into" reality according to its formal aspect. It is nothing less than "what the thing is," enlivening and moving the intellect, uniting it to the real precisely according to that which "realizes" the real. It is therefore genuine intuition; it is *seeing in* the thing precisely that which makes it to be what it is.

Conceptualization or simple apprehension is for Thomism only the beginning of the knowing process. Concepts are compared, joined together or distinguished from one another, and thus clarified in a discursive process which yields propositional judgments. Once again, Maritain stresses that the formation of *propositions* by the mind is not a mere notional exercise in logical association or ideological schematization. Rather it is a process by which intellectual intuitions that apprehend—in "simple perceptions"—the formal features of things become more precise, more developed, more distinguished *in light of* the "primordial intuition" that is co-extensive with experience as such—the intuition of being and its most inescapable and basic characteristics (the "first principles"). In the second operation of the mind, the judgment expressed in a proposition, we have once again—according to Maritain—an intellectual intuition, a simple perception of the intelligibility of a thing or of the relationships between things. In judgment, the process of analyzing concepts in the light of those fundamental principles which reflect the ontological structure of all things is resolved into a unified expression by the mind. The judgment is the mind dynamically actualized by a unified relationship of concepts through which it perceives—once again, but this time with a clarity proper to the full exercise of intelligence—things according to their inherent intelligibility.[46]

Here we would do well to note that Maritain uses the word "intuition" in several different ways. He proposes a basic distinction between "intuition in the strict sense" and "intuition in the broad sense". The former refers to "a knowledge without any intermediary or mean, even subjective."[47] The latter, however, can be taken to mean "a knowledge without *objective* intermediary, that is to say which directly attains its object without interposition of another term or object first known."[48] Maritain notes that "intuition in the strict sense" was what the ancients meant by intuition; it was meant to refer to a direct and proper "seeing" of the object according to the way in which it is immediately present to the knowing power. Intuition in the strict sense pertains to Divine and angelic self-knowledge

---

[46] See *BergPhil*, pp. 104-105. "Then, at the end of the search the intellect knows again by a vital act, by a *dictio verbi*; it grasps the real by a "*simple perception*" expressed in a judgment (*secunda mentis operatio*) and one which restores to unity the at-least-virtual complexity discovered in the object" (p. 105).
[47] *BergPhil*, p. 149 fn.
[48] ibid.

and to the beatific vision; in these instances "the intellect is informed '*immediately*' by the essence or the substance of the thing known." It also pertains to the direct knowledge of things in their very singularity which the angels possess by virtue of the Divine illumination which actualizes the angelic intellect. And, finally, it pertains to human sense perception. In sensation there is no "expressed species" generated by the sense power as an instrument of its activity; rather the object itself—physically present to the sense power and active upon it—immediately actualizes the sense power to perceive it. Thus human sensation constitutes the basic human mode of experiencing "intuition in the strict sense"—the very notion of "intuition" is understood in terms of "seeing," because sight is the most vivid and developed form of intuitive sense knowledge.[49]

Maritain uses "intuition in the broad sense" to refer simply to direct perception—knowledge that really attains things in themselves. He justifies this extension of terminology as a response to modern epistemology's misunderstanding about the true nature of the concept. Since Descartes, the prevailing conviction among philosophers has been that the idea or concept as such is what is known; reality at best is attained only indirectly, and a truly critical philosophy must (if it can!) justify the "link-up" between the ideas known by the mind and the reality "behind them". Maritain has noticed that philosophers like Bergson, who view the concept as an artificial construction of the mind and who hunger and thirst for a genuine perception of the real, often develop more or less vague theories of "intuition" in an attempt to do an "end run"

---

[49] *BergPhil*, p. 150 fn.

around what appears to be so much obstructive mental furniture. These philosophers use the word "intuition" to describe some special epistemic process by which the mind reaches out dynamically and attains reality. Maritain thus wants to appropriate the term intuition insofar as it expresses modern aspirations to attain "direct perception," so as to say to the modern mind, "conceptualization is the intuition you're looking for!"[50]

At first glance, it might seem that Maritain's reference to conceptual knowledge as intuition is merely an apologetical device. His overall analysis, however, indicates that the issue is more than semantic. By extending the use of the term "intuition," Maritain is led to underscore certain features of human knowing that were perhaps overly neglected in previous scholastic treatises. Maritain insists that "intuition in the broad sense" bears at least some of the key characteristics of intuition in its fullest and most proper sense.

Maritain distinguishes two types of "intuition in the broad sense". The first is the "introspective perception of the self". In the process of knowing objects by conceptualization the mind has a direct experience of its own activity. The soul, by experiencing its own operations, thus recognizes its own existence; it has an experimental knowledge of its own presence and activity. This knowledge, Maritain says, can be called intuitive in the broad sense. It is properly intuitive in that it is an unmediated apprehension of a singular object according to its actual existence. It falls short of strict intuition,

---

[50] *BergPhil*, pp. 150-151 fn.

however, in that it is not a direct knowledge of the whatness of the individual soul, but only of its existence.[51]

The second type (to which Maritain devotes the bulk of his attention in *La Philosophie Bergsonienne*) is "intellectual perception" through concepts and judgments. Intellectual perception is properly intuitive because it is a direct contact with reality in its formal aspect, according to the intelligibility that things really and truly possess by virtue of the principles which constitute them. The vital, ordered, and purposeful character of the thing is "attained *directly* thanks to the idea (*species expressa*), which is only a term *quo* or *in quo* ('formal sign')." The idea "is not *that which* the intellect knows (the idea itself is known only by reflection), it is only *that by which* the intellect knows, that by which the intellect communicates with reality, that by which it grasps 'intuitively,' immediately, natures, objects of thought which are in things and which it brings forth from things by abstraction."[52] This intellectual perception falls short of strict intuition, however, because it does not know things directly in the very singularity of their actual existence; it knows directly only the formal aspect of things—those characteristics which are universal, which constitute their defining identities, their "natures".

Maritain concludes that this kind of intuition—the intuition of direct intellectual perception—characterizes

---

[51] *BergPhil*, pp. 150-151. Maritain explores further this fascinating "intuition" of the existence of one's own soul, and how it might constitute a means of a formally natural "mystical" experience of God by way of negation. See his essay "The Natural Mystical Experience and the Void," in *Ransoming the Time*, trans. Harry Lorin Binsse (New York: Charles Scribner's Sons, 1946), pp. 255-289, esp. beginning at 266.

[52] *BergPhil*, p. 151.

The Created Person and the Mystery of God

man's knowledge of things in the world. The human mind is able to see directly the natures of corporeal things that impact upon the senses, by means of the dynamic activity through which the mind lives within its own immaterial reality the intelligible forms of those things. To this whole order of direct intellectual perception, however, Maritain contrasts another order of knowing—an *in*direct perception in which certain realities are known only by means of other realities. Here we have a true *objective* mediation which excludes any type of "intuition". This is knowledge "by analogy". Here the mind is led to infer something about an object which it does *not* directly perceive, on the basis of *the relationship* between that object and another object which the mind does directly perceive. The object directly known thus serves as an intermediary for an analogical knowledge of another object which it resembles in some way. By means of this analogical knowledge—this indirect, non-intuitive, objectively mediated knowledge—"every created spirit knows God naturally through creatures, as in a mirror."[53]

The natural human intellect arrives at certitude concerning the *existence* of God through a process of reasoning that begins with aspects of reality directly accessible to "intellectual intuition". It then considers these factors in light of the implications of its own primordial

---

[53] ibid. For a fuller treatment of what Maritain terms "ananoetic intellection," see *Degrees*, pp. 218-226. See also pp. 226-231 for a more specific account of how analogy functions in our natural knowledge of God. God possesses positive attributes *formaliter-eminenter*–i.e. not only in a mode superior to the created analogues which mirror those attributes, but also in a way that is free from "the delimitations which distinguish them and without which I, myself, cannot conceive them." This explains how it can be that "all the Divine perfections are strictly identified in God" (p.227).

"intuition of being" (which, Maritain stresses in *la Philosophie Bergsonienne*, can be identified with the intuition of first principles), and is led to judge the existence of a *relationship* between those realities directly perceived and an unseen Cause that accounts for their being and movement, perfection and purposefulness.

In this reasoning process (as in every other reasoning process), we see the key role played by what Maritain refers to as the "intuition of being," particularly what might be called the intuition of being in the general sense, i.e. the implicit awareness of being that arises in the mind along with any intellectual engagement of particular things (including that informal rational process which Maritain terms "common sense"). This phrase "intuition of being" refers to a trademark of Maritainian thought, and in its *strict* sense it involves a fully explicit perception of being as such. In this way it constitutes the intellectual foundation for metaphysics as a specific science. In his critique of Bergson, Maritain does not propose the full scope of his theory of the intuition of being.[54] He is primarily interested here in the relationship between the "general" intuition of being and the knowledge of "first principles." Therefore he stresses the fact that "the idea of being...is the objective light of all our knowledge." He goes on to explain that "in this idea of being the intellect grasps intuitively, that is immediately and without discourse, the first principles of reason." He enumerates these as the principles of identity

---

[54] Maritain elucidates his theory of the metaphysical intuition of being in the third lecture of *A Preface to Metaphysics* [original edition 1931].

(non-contradiction), sufficient reason, causality, finality, and substance.[55]

This presentation of the relationship between the "idea of being" (which is the "objective light" of knowledge) and the first principles of reasoning is interesting. The intuitive character of the first principles rests on the fact that they delineate aspects of the idea of being; they express the invariable, "transcendental" characteristics of being. These characteristics are seen immediately in the simple and fundamental recognition of being that rises up *first* in the intellect when it encounters the world. Everything else is known and understood, affirmed or denied in relation to this primordial perception.

Thus the intellect is led to affirm God's existence under the light of the intuition of being. The mind apprehends different aspects of the being and activity of things it knows directly—for example, the reality of change, of motion, of the actualization of potentiality. Things *become* what they were not before. When the intellect considers the reality of change in light of its primordial intuition of first principles, it is led to look for a *sufficient explanation* for the changes in things, a *cause* of change. The fact of becoming, which the intellect perceives directly, requires an adequate explanation. The same is true with regard to the phenomena of causality, contingency, perfection, and purposefulness: "in any case and in any way, it is because things are, and because they are in such a way that their being is not sufficient of itself, it is by their being that things make us know the existence of God; and it is thanks to the intellectual intuition of being, it is by means of the

---

[55] *BergPhil*, p. 127.

principle of identity and the principles which are linked to this supreme principle, it is by that sole means, primordially implied in the natural play of intelligence, that our reason raises itself to God."[56]

Maritain opposes what he thinks is an implication of Bergson's thought, namely, that the vital intuition of evolving reality leads—in its most intensified moment—to an intuition of the Divine, creative matrix from which all actualization emanates. Maritain, however, not only rejects the attainment of the Divine by Bergsonian intuition. He insists that no form of natural intuition (strict or broad) can attain the reality of God. Natural human intelligence transcends the physical objects of the universe only through an indirect, analogical mode of knowing. Natural intellectual intuition grasps the natures and properties of corporeal beings. In so doing, the intellect is capable of recognizing that the objects it knows have their being and activity, their natures and characteristics, *on account of Something Else* that the intellect does not know directly. The direct perception of the limited being, perfection, and intelligibility of things leads the intellect to affirm indirectly (by analogy) an Unlimited Being, Perfection, and Intelligibility that is the source of and ultimate explanation for the things we know. For natural intelligence, however, such an affirmation is carried beyond the world only on the wings of analogy. God is in no sense directly perceived by natural intelligence, because "of the infinite distance between the divine nature and our own." Intuitive knowledge of God is not accessible to any metaphysical effort, says Maritain. Rather, such direct perception of the

---

[56] *BergPhil*, p. 185.

Divine essence can only come by means of "the most supernatural gift of His mercy, that which constitutes, according to St. Thomas, our very beatitude."[57]

It is interesting to note the mention Maritain makes at this point of the role "the heart, the will, the experience of life" play in leading to a "practical conviction" of the existence of God. The convincing character of these approaches is founded on the way in which they are pervaded by the operation of the intellect, albeit spontaneous and unreflective. Maritain wants to register his opposition to those who *limit* natural knowledge of the existence of God to the practical divinations that result from "the profound sentiment of our indigence, and the need for order, and the desire for good," etc. He insists that these practical certitudes have "persuasive force only because the intelligence...comes into play unawares, under cover of feeling and moral aspirations, and starts at least somehow returning to the instinctive proofs of common sense,—which are but philosophical demonstrations in the implicit state."[58]

---

[57] *BergPhil*, p. 191. For an explanation of the distinctions between the strictly human analogical knowledge of natural theology, the "superanalogous" knowledge of faith (in which Divinely chosen analogues are used to mediate knowledge of God's inner essence, an object entirely inaccessible to natural reason and yet still–in faith–known only indirectly through the analogies of Divine revelation), the quasi-experiential knowledge of mysticism (supernatural not only according to its object but also according to its mode [the affective movement of supernatural charity], but still not *intellectually direct* knowledge), and finally the direct fullness of the Beatific Vision (in which God is finally known directly, since in the Beatific Vision man "knows Him by and in His very essence..., according to what He is in Himself, in a way proportionate to what He is, without the mediation of any creature or concept.") see *Degrees*, pp. 247-253.

[58] *BergPhil*, p. 192.

In Maritain's critique of Bergson, however, subjective experiences are to be taken seriously only because the inchoate work of the intelligence accompanies them. There is no suggestion here that a "profound sentiment of our indigence" or of "the need for order" or of "the desire for the good" or of "the effort of the whole soul, living and acting" (a phrase which Maritain borrows from Laberthonnierre) can *in their own right* act as subjective means of knowing (fulfilling a role analogous to the concept—as actualizations within the soul through which the reality of the object is engaged). Maritain here has not yet developed his more mature position on the possibility of "pre-philosophic" knowledge by ways of inclination.[59] It is worth noting, however, that Maritain, from the very

---

[59] Maritain expands his consideration of the role of inclinations in certain types of knowing processes when he turns his consideration to the realm of moral philosophy. It is necessary to recognize that, for the ordinary person, "in the case of moral values…we are in the presence of a rational knowledge which is implicit and preconscious and which advances, not by the mode of reason or concepts, but by the mode of inclination." A correct moral awareness, however, corresponds to those inclinations which proceed from our rational nature. These inclinations are "born of *reason*, or rather of nature as grafted with reason." But in the fundamental basics of ordinary moral life "our intelligence does not judge by virtue of inferences and conceptual connections, by proofs and logical constraints; it judges in a non-conceptual way, by conforming to the inclinations within us…Its judgment has an implicitly rational value which is not disengaged as such." Nevertheless this rational character is present because these inclinations spring from our rational nature and therefore conform to rational purposes. See *Neuf Lecons sur Les Notions Premieres de la Philosophie Morale* (Paris: Tequi, 1950). We are quoting from the English translation *An Introduction To The Basic Problems Of Moral Philosophy*, trans. Cornelia N. Borgerhoff (Albany, NY: Magi Books, 1990), pp. 51-62. Also, Maritain explores other practical modes of non-conceptual "knowing" in the development of his aesthetics, as we shall see below.

beginning of his intellectual career, recognizes that an experience in the realm of inclination can stand "in the place of" the concept as a means of knowledge in the *supernatural* order. The inclination of charity perfected by the gift of wisdom produces a genuine "experimental knowledge of God" which, for all of its inadequacy, is understood to be mediated by the movement of supernatural love itself.[60]

At this early stage of his philosophy, however, Maritain does not seem prepared to extend this type of knowledge to the natural order.[61] The role of inclinations in the natural order is *not* to mediate non-conceptual, experimental knowledge of any significance, but rather simply to accompany, stimulate, and render more vivid the spontaneous and common sense operations of natural intelligence. Maritain expresses it thus:

> "in many people the life of reason is so feeble that rational perceptions most efficacious in themselves and most certain have need of a sort of reinforcement by motives of sentiment and practice less removed from the life of the senses and acting precisely in the way of *sensitizers*. But it is nevertheless the life of the reason, however

---

[60] See *BergPhil*, p. 191 fn.

[61] In his later work *Approaches to God* (to which we have already alluded), Maritain devotes an entire chapter to "existential and pre-philosophic" *ways* in which the practical intellect approaches God, both in the aesthetic order and in the moral order.

> hidden it may sometimes be, which here again
> plays the essential role."[62]

It should here be noted that Maritain's view of common sense reason acting within the context and under the stimulus of subjective experience has a validity in itself, and indeed is probably the path that most of us follow (it seems to me that, for most of the human race, reason is "so feeble" and hence in need of the process Maritain describes). In any case, it certainly seems to be an apt description of a particular kind of psychological process by which many human beings arrive at the conviction of God's existence.

As we have said, by analogy the human being is naturally capable of reasoning to a certitude about the existence of God. Analogous reasoning also affords an indirect but genuine knowledge of the Divine attributes—known by means of created things which "reflect" the Divine nature. This is true especially of those characteristics which all things share simply in virtue of the fact that they are beings. Unity, truth, goodness—the "transcendental" facets of being which each thing possesses according to its own essential manner—are co-extensive with being as such, and are therefore *proper* to the Divine being, although in a *manner* unknown to us.[63]

In *La Philosophie Bergsonienne* Maritain outlines the basic features of classical Thomistic natural theology, but with a more dynamic emphasis. Maritain stresses that the mental word is the actualization of the intellect by the

---

[62] *BergPhil*, p. 192

[63] *BergPhil*, p. 195. See also *Degrees*, pp. 226-231, as noted above (footnote 53).

formality inherent in things, and *through* this mental word the intelligibility of things is directly perceived in a manner which is worthy of being called "intellectual intuition." The most basic of all intellectual intuitions is the intuition of being, which arises—at least in its initial form—at the root of every act of knowledge, and which expresses itself within the mind in terms of those principles which are evidently involved in the very structure of being. In the light of this primordial intuition the mind delineates its concepts, relates them, and judges them—living at every stage of the mental process a vital contact with the real. This intuitive vitality pertains to the whole realm of reality which is proportioned to the human intellect, that is, the realm of the physical universe. The human mind, however, is capable of transcending the physical objects proportioned to it—not by a more profound or concentrated intuition, but by a different way of knowing—"analogous" intellection, which leads the mind from directly perceived effects to their indirectly (yet certainly) inferred Transcendent Cause.

[2] Maritain on the Will and its Orientation Toward God

La Philosophie Bergsonienne serves as a kind of "handbook" of Maritain's early philosophical thought, which has particular value for the way in which it opens up new vistas in classical Thomist realism. Having examined therein the account of the operation of intelligence, it is worthwhile to turn to its treatment of the will, as well as to other texts which augment and complete the basic outline of Maritain's view of the will.

The human will is "the appetite which follows upon intelligence;" therefore, just as the object which corresponds to the intellectual power is *being*, so the object which corresponds to the will is that same being considered under its transcendental aspect of value, of worthiness, of that which characterizes being as able to be *possessed* by a spiritual person—in a word, being as *good*. The will is distinguished as a faculty—a spiritual power—by the good as such. Therefore says Maritain, following the whole Thomistic tradition, the will cannot choose evil for its own sake. Moreover, the will *necessarily* wills, "from the instant it exercises itself," that *ultimate aim* which is coextensive with its essential orientation—the good in its total and complete sense, "good in all its fullness, universal good, absolute good, unmixed good, beatitude."[64] Thus Maritain expresses the classical Thomistic conviction about the Final End as the object which necessarily determines the whole scope of the will. Thus also Maritain identifies the basis of *freedom* (in the sense of the will's *indifference*—its "dominating indetermination") with reference to all

---

[64] *BergPhil*, pp. 267-268.

particular goods. If the adequate object of the will—the only object which exhaustively corresponds to its spiritual dynamism and engages it necessarily—is absolute, unlimited goodness, it follows that every object that falls short of absolute goodness (every "particular good" which participates in goodness only to a certain extent) will not engage the will necessarily, and will be chosen (or not chosen) by the will only with reference to and "for the sake of" the ultimate good.

Maritain distinguishes three ways in which *the good* exercises its attraction on the human will: (1) the "good as end in itself" (bonum honestum) which interests the will on account of "the perfection it includes and which makes it desirable in itself;" (2) the "useful good, which is only a *means*," that is, it interests the will only insofar as it enables the will to attain another good; (3) "the *delectable good*, which is only an effect or a repercussion of the possession of a good", of a bonum honestum—"*rest* in the good possessed."[65]

In his description of the relationship between intellect and will in the genesis of a *free act*, Maritain draws a fundamental and important distinction between the *speculatively practical* judgment ("speculativo-pratique") and the *practically practical* judgment ("practico-pratique"). The first bears upon practical matters as to its content, but is speculative as to its form; it judges what must be done in particular circumstances by analyzing the nature of those circumstances as related to the universal norms and exigencies of the good. The second bears upon practical matters in a singular fashion, in light of the

---

[65] *BergPhil*, p. 267 fn.

concrete, living relationship between the exigencies and inclinations of my own will, and the absolute good. Maritain insists that it is only the second judgment (the "practically-practical" judgment) that "determines" the will—that provides the "sufficient reason," the explanation, the "why" of its act. This judgment, however, is made in light of the free inclination of the concrete will, of "my" will.[66]

As we have seen, the will is moved *necessarily* only by Absolute Goodness as such; only the "call" of pure, perfect, unlimited Goodness can bind the will, and it does so in the measure in which it is present as object of the will, exercising its influence upon it. None of the particular goods presented to the will by the intellectual apprehension of beings in the world are Goodness-As-Such. All of these goods interest the will only insofar as the foretaste of Absolute Goodness is present within them, and insofar as they suggest themselves as means, as pathways, to the attainment of the Good. Now the intellect is capable of making a speculative judgment—a judgment corresponding to the objective truth of things (*per conformitatem ad rem*)—about what *should be done* in a particular situation, based on its perception of the objective relationship between particular circumstances and the Universal Good. This is the speculatively practical judgment. Notice, however, an important feature of this judgment. Although the intellect here recognizes the objective links between a certain particular good and the Ultimate Good, although it

---

[66] See *BergPhil*, pp. 269-274. As we will observe further below, here we see already the idea of a practical "knowledge by inclination" that Maritain will develop in a much broader sense in his moral philosophy (see, e.g., *Moral Philosophy*, cited above [footnote 59]).

recognizes that a human being should do this action in this set of circumstances in order to move toward the attainment of goodness, and although the intellect even recognizes that, since *I* am a human being and I am in these circumstances, it follows—through the logic of speculative reasoning—that *I* should do this action, *still* the reality that is actually, concretely present to the will is a partial, limited good. The thing which is here and now exercising its attractive force on my will is not, here and now, the Absolute Good which alone corresponds totally to my will. Therefore, the speculatively-practical judgment of "what is to be done" cannot, of itself, *determine* the will.[67]

The will requires a more concrete perception of the particular good. Maritain expresses it thus: "the act that I have to do is a concrete and particular act; it is not a human act in general, nor an act of my own simply determined as human; it is essentially an act of *mine, determined as my own*. The will requires of the intellect, in order to be determined to such an action, *a decree which bears in particular on that action as my own*, as a concrete and singular act relating to my end and to my personal and singular will of my end."[68] It is through the will's own free inclination toward the particular good that this practically-practical judgment is made. In effect, the intellect formally determines the will's concrete act by judging the relationship between a particular option and Goodness-as-such that the will itself establishes for itself by virtue of its own inclination, its own active "preference". Thus, in the practically-practical judgment, the intellect judges the

---

[67] ibid.
[68] *BergPhil*, pp. 269-270.

"place" (so to speak) that a particular good occupies in relation to the will's own dynamic inclination; "it judges, *in relation to the will*, that a certain partial good is *hic et nunc* the means of absolute good."[69] And it makes this judgment because the will, "by virtue of its inclination toward one or other of the alternatives, applies the intellect to judge."[70] The intellect's judgment "determines" the will, exercises formal causality in specifying the nature of a human act, *only* as a consequence of the will's "already" *moving*, inclining toward the particular good in its freedom. The will is formally specified by the intellect only because it—of itself and by virtue of its own dynamism—"proceed[s] toward a certain specification to be received." In this the will is *efficient cause* of the intellect's practically-practical judgment, even while the intellect formally determines the will's act. And although both causalities operate simultaneously in the synergy of "that instantaneous operation which constitutes the act of free will," the efficiency of the will is metaphysically "prior"—it is the essential and foundational source of the act. Maritain states that it is this free inclination of the will which is responsible for "*making* of a certain particular good the very means, signified *hic et nunc*, of the perfect good it naturally wills." The intellect's judgment is "*per conformitatem ad appetitum*"—it is a judgment about what is "already" "in" the will.[71]

---

69 *BergPhil*, p. 272 fn

70 *BergPhil*, p. 272.

71 ibid. As Maritain explains elsewhere, the role of the will is crucial in the determination of the sinful character of an action. The origin of the fault of sin is in the will's inclining toward a particular good without regard for the proper ordination of goods and of the rational order of human inclinations as

Maritain does not explain here how the will "makes" the particular good into the will's own means of the absolute good, but it is not difficult to see here the beginnings of the suggestion of a non-conceptual, incommunicable, subjective "knowledge" that occurs through the mediation of the inclination of the will as such (indeed, this kind of "knowledge" plays an important role in Maritain's moral philosophy, as we have already seen). Maritain notes that "the *singular will itself* that the subject has of his own absolute good...plays the part of major premise in the syllogism of the practically practical judgment."[72] It is difficult to see how something could "play the part of major premise" without being in some sense, in and of itself, "knowledge". Here, however, Maritain is only concerned with how this inclinational knowledge—this wholly personal, wholly subjective perception of *my* good—stands

---

grasped in the concrete perception of the natural law. This Maritain refers to as "the voluntary non-consideration of the rule." This "non-consideration" is not in itself an act; rather it is a defect in the will's inclination and is the source of the defective, "evil" character of the action which follows. It is, nevertheless, a voluntary defect, a failure of freedom in its operation, a falling-away from the measure of reason which the free will permits within itself, thus introducing not a "something" but a *nothing*, an absence of actuality that vitiates the inclination, thereby distorting the intellect's practico-practical judgment and the will's free *act*. For a thorough treatment of these points, see *Existence and the Existent* (New York: Pantheon, 1948), pp. 85-122. See also Maritain's Marquette lecture of 1942, "St. Thomas and the Problem of Evil" (Milwaukee: Marquette University Press, 1942). Maritain's fascinating study *The Sin of the Angel* [trans. William L. Rossner, S.J. (Westminster, MD: The Newman Press, 1959)] is a careful examination of various issues that arise in connection with the nature of created freedom.

[72] *BergPhil*, p. 270 fn.

as major premise for the practically-practical judgment of the intellect which specifies the free act.

In light of the foregoing reflections, it is worthwhile to note a few points that Maritain makes in *La Philosophie Bergsonienne* about the "natural desire" for God. When he says that the will necessarily wills "universal good, absolute good, unmixed good...the good which saturates all desire," Maritain draws a distinction—in a footnote—"between *felicity* or *happiness in general*, to which the human will tends necessarily by virtue of a natural desire, and *absolute happiness* or *beatitude*, to which it tends necessarily by virtue of a trans-natural desire."[73] Here Maritain simply cites this distinction without answering (or even raising) the very interesting question of how a "trans-natural desire" fits into the structure of necessary volition. Maritain then continues with the assertion that the will's essential dynamic toward Goodness-as-such, and its essential indetermination with reference to "all goods [that] are not *the* Good", implies an essential, non-cognized desire for God: "for where is pure good in reality, if not in subsisting Good itself? That is why every will, even the most perverse, desires God without knowing it."[74]

The natural desire of the will for the absolute, pure Good is a natural desire for God that is "unaware" of the specific object corresponding to it. The will does not *directly* aim at God as the proper and distinct object of its inclination; it cannot be said that God, as a transcendent reality distinguished from the whole universe of being, is "already" properly inscribed in the will's inherent tendency. Also,

---

[73] *BergPhil*, p. 268.
[74] ibid.

Maritain makes it clear that the natural desire for the universal good arises *only when the will exercises itself* (the will "cannot, from the instant it exercises itself, not will an ultimate aim"). Moreover, this desire (arising as it does when the will *exercises* itself) follows upon the intellectual apprehension of "being"—it is the extent, the scope, of the movement of the intellectual appetite, "going out" to embrace the whole universe of reality as perceived "first" by the intellect. The "necessary" movement of the will follows that fundamental intellectual intuition of being which is at the foundation of every properly intellectual apprehension of the realities of the world. Just as the light of the intellect makes "being" stand out (in its most basic and general sense—what the scholastics call *ens commune*) as the common feature of realizability and intelligibility characteristic of every object experienced or imagined in sense cognition, so also the intellect presents "being" to the will according to the transcendental feature which makes being (all being insofar as it *is* being) worthy of possession, "valuable," *good*: "it is therefore the good in its typical form or value as intelligence makes it stand out from the shadows of sensible goods, let us say *pure good*" that the will necessarily desires when it is awakened by an encounter with the universe of being.[75]

When it meets the world of good things, the will inclines toward this or that thing on account of the goodness it possesses; and this implies that a more fundamental inclination has been born within the will, an inclination coextensive with willing as such, an inclination toward goodness in its formal aspect. And because only God

---

[75] *BergPhil*, p. 267.

possesses Goodness in its purely formal mode, we must say that the will's desire for formal goodness is a desire for God. However, the recognition (the *knowledge*) that God is the ultimate aim necessarily desired by the will only comes at the conclusion of a process of metaphysical reasoning, wherein the Divine attribute of absolute Goodness is inferred from the analogous character of "the good" and its limited instantiation in all directly perceivable things. Although Maritain does not simply state this classical Thomistic thesis, he affirms it by carrying out just such a process of metaphysical reasoning in order to complete his analysis of the will's natural desire for God.[76]

In subsequent texts, Maritain will take up more specifically the various distinctions between the will's intrinsic, natural ordination toward God as end (known indirectly in His effects), the will's "trans-natural" desire that man might see directly the essence of the God who is known indirectly, and the will's *de facto* ordination to Beatitude, a union with God that can only be achieved within an order superior to nature, an order that God has in fact constituted as man's existential situation.

According to Maritain, the happiness proportionate to the natural man would be a "happiness in motion," an essentially imperfect fulfillment consisting in "a natural contemplation and natural love of the world and of God progressing without end." This "felicity" would be *sufficient* for the realization of human nature, but it would not be the full realization of everything to which man could possibly aspire.[77] Thus we may speak of a "trans-natural"

---

[76] See *BergPhil*, pp. 268-269.
[77] *Moral Philosophy*, pp. 107-111.

The Created Person and the Mystery of God

desire that is proper to human nature, and this would be nothing less than the desire to see the essence of the God who makes us. It is clear that such a vision is utterly disproportionate to the capacities of human nature, or indeed of any created nature—hence the term "trans-natural".[78] According to Maritain, this desire—left unfulfilled—would not ruin the happiness proportionate to human nature, if in fact this happiness alone were the concrete destiny of man.[79] Nevertheless, because this trans-natural desire springs from "the very depths of the thirst of our intellect for being"—i.e. since it is rooted in our nature—-its fulfillment must be in some way possible. Clearly it is impossible for human nature to attain by its own power. "But it is necessary that by some means (which is not nature) it *be able* to be satisfied...In other words it is necessary that an order superior to nature be possible in which man is capable of that of which nature is incapable."[80] Thus the trans-natural desire to see the Divine essence indicates (in and of itself) the *possibility* of "an order superior to nature." Maritain distinguishes this from the specifically *supernatural order* (the order in which man participates in the Divine life), which is accessible only to faith. What man's trans-natural desire indicates is only that some kind of order superior to nature is *possible* and that "through the divine generosity man can therein be rendered capable of knowing God in His essence."[81] This inefficacious desire, "natural" to man and yet not necessary

---

[78] *Moral Philosophy*, pp. 111-112; *Approaches to God*, pp. 98-99.
[79] *Moral Philosophy*, pp. 111-112.
[80] *Approaches to God*, p. 99.
[81] ibid.

to his natural happiness, is radically capable of being fulfilled.

But what do we actually perceive about man's existential condition? What seems clear is that the concrete man is never satisfied with an imperfect fulfillment. Man as we actually find him lives out his life as a drama of seeking complete happiness, "beatitude"—a condition which is only possible if Goodness itself is not merely "naturally" loved "from a distance," but also seen and possessed (indeed, known and loved in an interpersonal relationship). Here Maritain suggests something not unlike the basic thesis of the "supernatural existential" as it was initially proposed by Karl Rahner.[82] In fact, the human desire for happiness has been "infinitized" by God's free decision to ordain man to supernatural Beatitude. Original grace, lost by the first man, has nevertheless left as an ineradicable mark the centrality and the urgency for man's life that a trans-natural desire be fulfilled. "If human nature was irremediably and conclusively infinitized by Christian grace, it had first been infinitized, irremediably and inchoately, by the grace in which the first man was created." Maritain explains further that "once grace [and here he mentions explicitly the grace of Adam]...and faith have been given to the human species, we find ourselves infinitized, even if later we lose grace, and even if we lose faith." This is because the grace and the faith given to the first man produced a permanent effect on the human race: "the fixation or stimulation of the

---

[82] See Rahner's essay "Concerning Nature and Grace," in *Theological Investigations*, vol. I (Baltimore: Helicon Press, 1951).

transnatural desire for beatitude and of the transnatural desire to see the First Cause...remains in nature."[83]

This brief sketch of some elements of Maritain's philosophy of freedom and the will make clear the will's orientation toward Goodness-as-such, which in fact can only be found in God. Thus the will is ordered to God as man's ultimate good. The specific character of this ordination is more complex, however, and Maritain in the end is not afraid to turn to revelation in order to shed light on man's experience of restlessness with finite things, and the urgency of his desire for a relationship with the Infinite God.

Nevertheless Maritain's basic philosophical account of the will's ordination to Goodness-in-itself is not entirely satisfying. The will's seeking of the Good in every particular good is a desire for God that is unaware of its true object, unless that object has been particularly perceived and presented to the will by reason. This certainly presents a correct metaphysical framework for the issue, but perhaps what is missing is the psychological/phenomenological dimension: how is this ordination of the will to Goodness Itself experienced by man? This question, of course, brings us immediately into the thickets of the nature/grace problem, and the existential realm of actual experience. I hesitate, therefore, to try to pose the problem in what might seem to be "abstract" terms, but we must face the fact that, despite strenuous effort, theology has simply not resolved the problem of the relationship between nature and grace and the relationship between the final end proportionate to man's "nature" and the final end to which man has in fact

---

[83] *Moral Philosophy*, pp. 116-118.

been ordained by the free decision of God. Certain parameters have been identified which are understood by all orthodox Catholic theologians to be necessary consequences of revealed truth. Many interesting opinions have been proposed within these parameters, and the discussion—carried out widely in the 1940s and 1950s—has re-emerged in recent years as it has become clear that Vatican II's teaching on the relationship between the "mystery of Christ" and the "mystery of man" still leaves open many explanatory details in theology.

Raising the question, then, of how man "would have" experienced the "natural ordination" of his will to the Perfect Good "if" man had not been ordained to a supernatural end may seem like excessive scholastic hair-splitting. It may also be phenomenologically impossible to determine, since the de facto experience of man (which is all we have to reflect upon) is shot through with the supernatural. I believe, however, that it is worth raising in an effort to clarify the *inherently* religious character of the human being. What seems to me important (and what seems lacking in Maritain's analysis) is that any orientation toward a "Perfect Good" that transcends the particular goods immediately available to man's free choice implies experientially that man is seeking something *mysterious*. Moreover, we should understand "the Good" in a full, ontologically adequate sense, i.e. not simply as something which satisfies a human appetite conceived in terms of *consumption*, but as intrinsic worthiness, objective *value* that deserves affirmation for its own sake. In this way, we will see that the trajectory of human desire toward the perfect good is not simply one of acquisition, but also one of openness, receptivity, wonder, and self-surrender. It is appropriate to speak of the will as the "rational appetite" but we must realize that the specification "rational" requires us to understand appetite in a unique sense, a sense *analogous* to what appear to be the purely possessive appetites of the sub-rational order. Rational indicates *personal*, and thereby indicates that this "appetite" is an orientation toward *relationship* with Goodness; it is a dynamism toward affirmation and self-donation as well as possession (indeed, possession itself also must be understood here in a distinctly personal sense).

Natural human desire is a reaching out for "particular goods" *for the sake of* the Good-as-such, which means that particular goods become mediators of a journey toward a mysterious reality that possesses the Supreme Worthiness, the Supreme Splendor, the Supreme Wonderfulness; and there is already an implicit hint in this journey that the ultimate object is what *makes* everything else to be good. The experience of a "partial good" must contain within itself at least implicitly an indication of a goodness received from Elsewhere. And if particular, created beings are really *signs*, as we argued in Part I, man can scarcely possess and relate to them in a serious manner without being touched (once again at least implicitly) by the image of what they signify. Thus the element of its "belonging to a (mysterious) Other" impresses itself upon man when he chooses any created good. Man is thus led, even in the "natural order," toward a Mystery that possesses everything, and therefore has in itself a transcendent, numinous value. Might we therefore even go so far as to conclude that the human will, by its very willing, implicitly seeks something *worthy of worship*?

In any case, the fact that man is immersed in the order of grace means that he is, concretely, a religious being. His life and his desires are affected in such a way that he cannot be happy with anything less than the infinite fulfillment of the Beatific Vision. The inescapable urgency of this orientation is, Maritain himself argues, a feature of the supernatural order. But Maritain also argues that the end proportionate to human nature as such (and therefore the end that man "would have had *if*" God had not destined man for supernatural Beatitude) is an essentially incomplete "happiness in motion" that contemplates God as reflected in creation and that has a trans-natural desire to see the essence of God. Natural happiness knows that it is possible (by virtue of God's power) for this trans-natural desire to be fulfilled but it does not cease to be happiness if the desire is not fulfilled. Is this an adequate theory? Once again, an analysis "from the inside" (if you will) of these metaphysical observations is important. Might one observe that man, left to his own human powers, would live a stronger psychological experience of the "seeking part" of his "happiness in motion" than of the "satisfied part"? If his contemplation of God is progressive and, in principle, can go on without end within its own order (that is, an order of indirect asymptotic progression), does that not seem to place the will in a position of "always wanting more" in this dynamic natural happiness? This is not because man's nature is defective qua nature, but rather because of the perfection of what the will is as a faculty, namely, a limitless openness to the entire range of possibilities for relationship with the Good. Man is therefore essentially a seeker in the presence of the Divine Mystery. And it is not only because of his trans-natural desire that man knows about the possibility of God taking the initiative and giving something to man; clearly the "purely natural" will of man--especially when man is explicitly aware of a personal Creator--would seek predominantly through *asking* (i.e. through "prayer") with the awareness of the infinite benevolence of the Divinity. This "natural prayer"--even if it were offered with reference to the fulfillment of the trans-natural desire—would not in itself constitute any kind of positive disposition for what we know by faith to be the "supernatural order." It would be prayer for "something more;" some further gift from the Infinitely Good Giver. Indeed, the man who possesses this "happiness-in-motion" as the definitive natural achievement of his life would be aware of the fact that everything is ultimately a gift from God.

There remains further the issue of the perdurance of man's trans-natural desire to see the essence of God in the midst of man's natural happiness-in-motion. Without the supernatural order, it would not be *necessary* for this desire to be fulfilled in order for man to attain to the purpose proportionate to his humanity. Still, how would this trans-natural desire situate itself within the overall dynamic of natural happiness. Is it a mere wish: "gee, it would be nice, but it really doesn't matter that much"? Maritain himself thinks otherwise: the desire to see the essence of God "is not a simple velleity, a superadded desire, a desire of supererogation. It is born in the very depths of the thirst of our intellect for being; it is a nostalgia so profoundly human that all the wisdom and all the folly of man's behavior has

Studies in the Thought of Jacques Maritain

in it its most secret reason."[84] The strength of this statement seems to indicate that the desire to see the essence of God would be a central feature of the life of "purely natural" man, and that even his happiness would be full of the awareness of the possibility that God might grant some kind of more profound vision of Himself as a gift. Nor does it seem too far fetched to hypothesize that natural man, with complete humility but also with that religious awareness that (I have argued) permeates the whole disposition of his being, would ask his distant but beneficent Creator to make possible this unimaginable fulfillment.[85]

In any case let us now leave the thin air of this hypothetical realm. I have probably dared too much in proposing modes of experience that can never be *actually* verified. Yet it does not seem entirely unreasonable to attempt to start from the inherent, structural capacities of a nature and its powers, and then try to "visualize" what their actions might be like under a certain set of imagined circumstances.

Still, reality is what concerns us. And Maritain has no doubts that the concrete human person—in the existential state in which God has in fact created him—has an ineradicable need for the total and infinite fulfillment of a relationship with God. The concrete man cannot be happy

---

[84] *Approaches to God*, p. 99. Maritain himself seems unsure how much "weight" to give to the trans-natural desire.

[85] Note here that natural man would not ask God for the "Beatific Vision" as such, since without grace and revelation he cannot know about the Trinity or participation in the divine life. Here once again, he would only be asking—in the strongest possible sense—for "more" in his relationship with the Infinite Good.

any other way. And, as Maritain indicates in this next study, the philosopher cannot ignore this *fact* about man.

[3] Maritain on Reason and Revelation

At the end of the first edition of *La Philosophie Bergsonienne*, Maritain devotes several important pages to the relationship between philosophical reasoning and the possibility of Divine Revelation.

Maritain restates "that solely by its own power human reason is capable of recognizing both the existence of God and several of the verities concerning Him." He continues, however, by listing the immense difficulties involved in the attainment of such a knowledge—the dangers, pitfalls, and occasions for error which constantly afflict the indigent human intellect when it probes the supreme objects of philosophical thought. It makes sense, therefore, for the philosopher to seek a more secure path in such matters, to seek enlightenment from sources stronger than his own intellect. Thus it seems that the philosopher—given the limitations of the conditions within which he exercises his intelligence—ought to be open to some form of "higher help," and therefore ought to be open to God's own self-testimony if it should happen to occur. Formally speaking, philosophical reasoning can attain to the existence and attributes of God. However, philosophical reasoning as practiced by weak (not to mention prejudiced, narrow, and distorted) human intellects is constantly a prey to error when it approaches the Object which—although Supremely intelligible in Itself—is infinitely distant from the human mind. Thus, "reason demands" that in dealing with the things of God, the philosopher ought to ascertain whether or not God has spoken in history. "If God has told us about Himself it is indispensable for us to have recourse to His testimony, even for the problems which philosophy is capable—but at what risk!—of solving by itself alone."[86]

At the same time, however, Maritain situates these reflections in a context broader than the exigencies of philosophy. After all, the philosopher is *a man*, and when he "arrives at the limits of philosophy"—when he "glimpse[s] the existence of a personal God"—he "becomes anxious to know God, and the relations of man to God." Maritain indicates that the philosopher, when he takes up "the study of divine things," is thrust into a realm of consideration that is both higher and broader—more fundamental—than philosophy itself: "it is no longer a question of philosophizing. It is a question of living or dying." Metaphysics leads us to the discovery of "a living and active God...the God of the whole man." At this point, Maritain asks the philosopher, "can you continue to deal with Him as a theorist does with an idea, and not as a man with his Lord? There are secrets which He alone can reveal. You yourself are one of these secrets. You would know your end and the means to attain it if you knew these secrets. But you will only know them if it pleases God to reveal them Himself."[87]

---

[86] *BergPhil*, p. 297. Maritain expands on this theme in an essay "La Liberté Intellectuelle," written in the same year (1914) as the first edition of *La Philosophie Bergsonienne* and reproduced as chapter 2 of *Antimoderne* (1922). "Pour employer le langage des théologiens, il faut dire que dans l'etat de nature dechue, la raison est capable "physiquement" de connaitre, avec ses seules forces, toute verite d'ordre naturel, mais qu'il ne lui est pas *moralement possible*, sans le secours d'une grace speciale ou de la revelation, de posseder, sans y meler l'erreur, l'ensemble de ces verites." From the second edition of *Antimoderne* (Paris: Editions de la Revue des Jeunes, 1922), p. 72.

[87] *BergPhil*, pp. 297-298.

A few distinctions expressed here are key. First of all, philosophical reasoning upon divine things—that part of metaphysics which is termed "natural theology"—is complete and internally coherent in its own formal line. Metaphysics, *as metaphysics*, can attain to an analogical knowledge of the existence and attributes of God. This distinction has important implications for understanding the proper ways of human intelligence. Maritain will insist, against Blondel, that metaphysics does not require supernatural revelation in order to be constituted formally as knowledge. Maritain's insistence on the need for the philosopher (*as philosopher*) to consult a possible Divine Revelation pertains not to a formal indigence on the part of metaphysics but rather to the circumstantial indigence of the weak human intellect that practices it. In subsequent works Maritain will develop in more detail his theory of how the data of revelation and theology aid, correct, and fecundate philosophical reasoning by helping it to *focus* on its own proper object.

At the same time, Maritain indicates that while metaphysics does not call for revelation in order to be formally complete in itself, metaphysics does impel the metaphysician into a realm of existential questions that only Divine revelation can answer. This is not because metaphysics *as* metaphysics terminates in unanswered questions, but rather because in metaphysics the object glimpsed, brushed against, by the intellect is That which is of supreme interest to the whole person. Thus it seems that "at the limits of philosophy" we do discover the still inadequately-answered *practical* questions: "what is my end and the means to attain it?" "Why are we born on this earth?" While philosophy reaches some analogical knowledge—formally complete within its own order—of the Ultimate Being, philosophy cannot tell us how intellectual appetite can come into relationship with the Ultimate Goodness whom this Being is. Metaphysics, by analogically clarifying this Object in the realm of speculative intelligence, only intensifies and clarifies the *questions* about that Object in the realm of practical intelligence.

Here Maritain is clear on the fact that man, in his actual state, *needs* Divine revelation. Man's experience indicates to him some important things: first of all, he is a bad metaphysician, obstructed in countless ways and by all manner of distractions in his aspiration to know the highest truths. Man is afflicted with a strange incompetence even with regard to things that should be within the reach of his natural powers; and not only the higher things (like metaphysics and such) but also the things pertaining to the ordinary business of living. Man needs help.

Also, experience indicates that man is made specifically for a destiny that he does not have the power to comprehend, and that the actual significance of his life evades him. There are echoes in the world that are suggestive of a transcendent destiny, but they are distorted--as if man once knew but now has lost the understanding of the purpose of his existence. He finds himself in the midst of a drama and does not know his part. The natural question which man asks in front of the universe and the mystery of his own being is intensified both by his own wounded condition and by the actual fact that the answer to this question is, by God's freely chosen design, something truly extraordinary. The existential man needs God to answer the question, "why was I created?"

[4] The Supernatural Approach to God: Maritain on Contemplative Experience.

We have seen that, according to Maritain, the human intellect's *natural* approach to God follows the indirect modality of analogous reasoning. Since there is no natural proportion between a created, finite intellect and the infinite, transcendent intelligibility of God, there can be no direct perception of God as the object of natural intellection. Maritain rejects any notion of a supreme intuition of the divine located at the natural summit of intellectual perception; the realm of natural intuition ("broadly" defined by Maritain to include the perception of the natures of things by the process of conceptualization) is restricted to the knowledge of creatures. Indeed, in the case of man it is limited to the objects of the physical universe (and to that one rather impoverished intuition that brushes against a spiritual object—the intuition man has of the *existence* of his own soul in action).

Analogous reasoning represents the limit of the natural capacity of the created intellect in the presence of the Supreme Object of metaphysics, a limit—moreover—of which the created intellect is aware, and which it has the (inefficacious) desire to surpass. In order to perceive God directly, however, the created intellect must transcend itself; it must be elevated to a new level of existence; it must be proportioned to the immensity of the Divine Mystery, and this proportioning can only be the effect of the Mystery Himself fashioning a divine-like capacity within the human soul. This new level of being, this proportioning of finite intellect to infinite intelligibility, constitutes the *supernatural* order.

The Created Person and the Mystery of God

At the summit of the supernatural order there is indeed a direct intuition of the Divine Essence—the Beatific *Vision* is, as we already pointed out, intuition in the strict sense. Short of the Beatific Vision, however, there remains a veil between the mystery of God and the spiritual eye of the created intellect. Even when it is illuminated by the grace of faith, the intellect continues to operate according to its natural mode of conceptualization. Hence the truths of faith continue to express the divine in analogous terms; the hidden mystery of God is known by faith, but this knowledge remains *in*direct. There is no question here even of "intuition in the broad sense," because no human concept or propositional judgment can possibly function as a "formal sign" of the Divine Essence. Recall that in Maritain's metaphysics of knowledge, the intellect is actualized by—it "lives" intentionally—the very formality of the thing that it knows. Such an intentional life, however, remains finite—it is the actualization of a *created* being, the created intellect. Even when a created intellect is actualized by the supernatural mysteries of faith, it can only "live" these mysteries according to created similitudes proportioned to itself—not according to their proper form which is the very infinite life of God. Hence in faith the hidden mystery of God is known not according to its own (infinite) proportions, but indirectly by means of a system of analogues coordinated and presented to human intelligence by the authoritative action of God within history.[88]

---

[88] Maritain develops the role of analogy in faith explicitly in *Degrees*, pp. 241-244.

Nevertheless, although there is no supernatural intuition of God short of the Beatific Vision, there is a genuine supernatural *experience* of God which goes beyond the analogous knowledge of faith. From the beginning of his intellectual career, Maritain gives significant attention to the realms of mysticism and contemplation. Here he confronts the emphasis of the Christian tradition on the whole exquisite domain of the interior life, the working of the Holy Spirit within the depths of the human soul, and the supernatural actualization of the human subject—above all through the will's inclination which is supernaturally wedded to God in the movement of charity.

In his great work *The Degrees of Knowledge*, Maritain weaves various elements of mystical theology into a systematic epistemology of supernatural contemplation.[89] This achievement requires a much more lengthy study than it is possible to set out here. But Maritain himself provides us with an outline of his systematic reflections in a small volume he co-authored with his wife Raissa in 1922, *La Vie D'Oraison*. Maritain observes the key features of mystical contemplation in the Christian tradition: (1) it is a kind of experimental knowledge of God; (2) it depends on the soul's affective union with God; (3) it transcends human conceptualization altogether, which is why the realm of natural intelligence can only describe it as "darkness" [even though it is—by its very nature—a superior kind of knowledge, which accounts for the paradoxical expressions used by the mystics to describe it, such as "luminous darkness"]; (4) it is a supernatural actualization of the

---

[89] This constitutes the whole second part of the study, "The Degrees of Suprarational Knowledge" (pp. 247-383).

intellect which is described in terms of "passivity". These features lead Maritain to conclude that contemplation is a kind of knowledge whose mode is both wholly supernatural (since it bypasses altogether the natural operation of the intellect—its natural mode of intentionally living the formality of its object through the expressed concept) and inclinational (since it is nevertheless still "by means of" something within the subject that God is attained—the dynamic of charity).[90]

Thus there is, in the supernatural order, an experimental attainment of God by the intellect, a knowledge "by a sort of connaturality" which is "affective," because it "depends essentially on charity." It is also "experimental" because charity unites the soul directly to God through the will and therefore institutes a proximity to the Divine mystery which energizes and suffuses the will's movement. Nevertheless, it must also be termed "obscure," because it does not touch any of the ordinary mechanisms (so to speak) of the intellective faculty—it leaves them behind because they are inadequate to the task at hand. Charity's direct taste of divine things is essentially superior to the indirect, analogical knowledge of the conceptualizing intellect.[91] In contemplation, the intellect thus appears "passive" because

---

[90] The first edition of *La Vie D'Oraison* was privately printed in 1922. Our citations are taken from the English translation, *Prayer and Intelligence*, trans. Algar Thorold (New York: Sheed & Ward, 1943), hereafter referred to as *Prayer*. Maritain states that contemplation is "union with God through an experimental, loving and ineffable knowledge of him" (*Prayer*, p. 17). It "raises man to a knowledge and love of God which are all spiritual...transcending the order of images and ideas and therefore incomprehensible and ineffable, and introducing the soul into the luminous cloud of divine things" (*Prayer*, p. 21).

[91] See *Prayer*, pp. 22-23.

it is passive with respect to its natural operations, and relies instead on the supernatural action of God which is present in the soul as drawing the soul's movement of love toward Him. In this way "infused contemplation gives the intelligence, passive under the action of God,...a knowledge more perfect than any distinct intellectual operation—a knowledge, indeed, entirely out of proportion with what we call knowledge on the plane of our senses and reason."[92]

In essence, Maritain's presentation here is in line with the mystical theology being developed by the Dominican school in the late 19th and early 20th centuries. It draws out the implications for epistemology of the mysticism of St. John of the Cross. Mysticism here is not a matter of extraordinary phenomena, visions, revelations, and such. Rather it is specifically Christian contemplation, where an "obscure" but at the same time much more profound knowledge of God is obtained through the experience of the will's movement of adherence to God in charity. This idea has far reaching implications. Since every Christian who is faithful to his baptism possesses charity, the possibility of an experience, and "encounter," with God concretely through the exercise of charity is perhaps much more

---

[92] *Prayer*, pp. 25-26. In *Trois Reformateurs* (1925), Maritain will apply his understanding of contemplation and the gifts of the Holy Spirit within the context of his critique of modern philosophy as a whole. Supernatural contemplation—by transcending rational processes—counters the ambitions and the frustrations of a supposedly self-sufficient modern reason. "There is a wisdom of the Holy Spirit higher above philosophic wisdom than heaven above earth, in which God is known and tasted not by distinct ideas, but by the connaturality of love proceeding from the union procured by charity." See the English translation *Three Reformers* (New York: Crowell, 1929), p. 40.

widespread than the term "mysticism" might indicate. Even if (as is perhaps mostly the case) this encounter is largely outside of the realm of consciousness (which is so taken up with other things), it can break through and have an impact on man's awareness, introducing something "new" and transforming into man's experience.

[5] The Theological Significance of the Experience of Beauty According to Maritain.

Any consideration of the value of human experience must take into account that special form of experience wherein man encounters the beautiful. Here Maritain has made a particularly important contribution to philosophy. We can only raise a few basic points here that relate to our consideration of man's relation to God.

The experience of the beautiful is distinguished by the fact that it has an *objective* character which enlightens the intellect while remaining concrete. In *Art and Scholasticism*, Maritain's preoccupation is with the *habitus* and operations associated with artistic creation. Nevertheless this concern leads him to an analysis of the perception of beauty—an experience which is concrete as to its mode and yet transcendental and metaphysical as to its object.

Maritain insists that beauty is a transcendental in the strong sense of the term: "it is being itself considered from a certain aspect...it is being considered as delighting, by the mere intuition of it, an intellectual nature."[93] Beauty characterizes every kind of being insofar as each being possesses formality, but beauty does not pertain to the formality of being considered as knowable (as to its content) by the intentionality of intelligence. Rather it pertains to formality in its sheer objective "radiance"; formality in its simple capacity to delight the intelligence

---

[93] See *Art and Scholasticism*, trans. J. F. Scanlan (New York: Charles Scribner's Sons, 1930), p. 24. Hereafter referred to as *Art*.

that encounters it even "before" the intellectual faculty begins to analyze it.

Maritain cites the scholastic definition of the beautiful: "id quod visum placet". The beautiful is that which gives joy on being "seen". As such, it is the object of intelligence. However, the proper effect of the beautiful is to delight the intelligence through the sheer recognition of the splendor of form; therefore the beautiful is attained through a concrete and direct experience rather than through any intellectual analysis. This is why Maritain insists that, for man, the experience of the beautiful involves a synergic interplay between intellect and sensation. Man experiences beauty when he recognizes the radiance of intelligibility glowing luminously within an object that engages his senses. The experience of the beautiful is characterized by an immediacy and a concreteness appropriate to intuition in the strict sense, therefore human aesthetics is necessarily linked to the only dimension of human cognition where such intuition takes place: sensation. In human aesthetic experience, the "brilliance of form, however purely intelligible it may be in itself, is apprehended *in* the sensible and by the sensible, and not separately from it...it is precisely through the apprehension of sense that the light of being penetrates to the mind."[94]

When it encounters the beautiful, the human mind rejoices in the splendor of being without going through the process of abstraction and conceptualization; it attains the object not through the mediation of its concept, but through the mediation of the sensible reality itself which directly informs sense intuition. In this attainment, the formality of

---

[94] *Art*, p. 21.

the thing does not in-form the intellect; rather it *delights* the intellect. Here the mind does not conform itself to the intelligible reality of the thing through a complete cognitive operation. Rather, the mind simply delights in the immediate recognition of the presence of intelligibility, of form, in the singular reality which has concretely engaged the senses.[95]

Aesthetic experience "is before all intellectual"—it really attains intelligibility, universality, the formal character of the thing—"and yet the apprehension of the universal or the intelligible takes place without...any effort of abstraction." The mind is moved by a perception of "glittering intelligibility" which is immediate because the object has been rendered proximate to the mind by sense cognition. This immediacy, however, not only bypasses abstraction and conceptualization; it precludes it. The experience of "the joy of the beautiful cannot be detached or separated from its matrix in the senses and consequently fails to procure an intellectual knowledge susceptible in practice of expression in a concept."[96] Thus the experience of beauty seems to involve a different modality of intellectual operation than the knowledge of a truth (which corresponds to the fact that beauty and truth are distinct transcendental aspects of being). In the case of truth, the

---

[95] The mind does not "extricate something intelligible from the matter in which it [i.e. the form] is buried and then step by step go through its various attributes." Rather, the mind, "fixed in the intuition of sense,...is irradiated by an intelligible light granted to it of a sudden in the very sensible in which it glitters; and it apprehends this light not *sub ratione veri*, but rather *sub ratione delectabilis*, by the happy exercise it procures for [the mind] and the succeeding joy in appetite, which leaps out to every good of the soul as its own peculiar object." *Art*, p. 21.

[96] *Art*, pp. 125-126.

The Created Person and the Mystery of God

mind through abstraction and conceptualization *understands something about* the formal character of a reality, something *about what it is*; whereas in the case of beauty the mind *simply recognizes the luminous presence* of form in its very informing of the particular reality, and *delights* in this recognition. The mind affirms, with a spontaneous immediacy, the goodness of the fact that something possesses form; the mind revels in the marvel of coherence. Thus, although the beautiful is experienced by the intellect, Maritain is inclined to place it more within the sphere of the good than of the true, and to characterize the intellectual modality through which the beautiful is perceived as a kind of accessory to the proper operation of the intellect which is ordered to the knowledge of truth: "the perception of the beautiful is related to knowledge, but by way of addition, 'as its bloom is an addition to youth'; it is not so much a kind of knowledge as a kind of delight."[97]

Maritain goes on to indicate that the transcendentality of beauty bestows theological significance upon the aesthetic experience. "Beauty…belongs to the transcendental and metaphysical order. For this reason it tends of itself to carry the soul beyond creation." It possesses a "theological quality," and indeed—when it is not integrated into the whole human dynamic toward the true and the good—it can exercise a "tyrannical spirituality" that pretentiously imitates the contours and the demands of holiness.[98] Nevertheless, the aesthetic experience seems to have some value in its own right as a *natural* approach to God, in that it attains, and causes delight in (and therefore awakens love

---

[97] *Art*, p. 21.
[98] *Art*, pp. 25-26.

for) a transcendental dimension of being which only God possesses in its fullness. The intellectual apprehension of the beautiful is a delight that tastes the image and likeness of the Divine Beauty. The aesthete is therefore "on the road which leads upright souls to God and makes invisible things clear to them by visible."[99] Maritain even notes "a remote analogy between the aesthetic emotion and the mystic graces", on account of the transcendentality, immediacy and extra-conceptuality of the attainment of beauty.[100]

All of this leads to the conclusion that Maritain does indeed recognize, in addition to the capacity of the natural intellect to attain truths of metaphysics and theodicy by means of its proper modality of operation (abstraction and conceptualization), a realm of *intellectual experience* in the natural order that aims the soul "beyond creation," and constitutes a kind of natural analogue for mystical experience. In the aesthetic experience, the intellect "seizes upon" an intelligible reality "without resorting to the concept as a formal means" and rejoices in the inherent splendor of intelligibility as suffusing the object of sense intuition—a "glittering" intelligibility "derived, like every intelligibility, in the last analysis from the first intelligibility of the divine Ideas", and therefore profoundly suggestive of its Source.[101] Maritain is not suggesting that the aesthetic experience provides a sort of natural intuition of the divine unavailable to conceptual intelligence. Aesthetic experience, through the intuition of the senses, directly attains the beauty of created beings, and—we might say—

---

[99] *Art*, p. 30.
[100] *Art*, p. 126.
[101] *Art*, pp. 30, 125.

only *indirectly* attains some foretaste of the Divine Beauty. However the implication seems to be that the aesthetic experience points in the direction of the Divine according to its own dynamic. Its "theological quality" is not derived from any conceptual process that accompanies it or operates covertly within it; Maritain has stated that aesthetic experience and conceptualization are mutually exclusive processes. Nor does its theological significance depend on any *subsequent* intellectual analysis which would identify and conceptualize the analogical relationship between created beauty and Uncreated Beauty. Rather, beauty "tends of itself to carry the soul beyond creation"—the reality of the analogy between Divine Beauty and created beauty proposes itself within the aesthetic experience, so that the soul is naturally drawn up by its grasp of the splendor of forms to at least desire that Splendor from which all else radiates. The process by which intellectual conceptualization is led from the objects directly proportioned to it to the analogical affirmation of Infinite Truth is perhaps paralleled within the concrete features of the experience of beauty, wherein the intellect—delighting in the beauty presented to it—is at the same time moved by an analogical presentiment and thirst for inexhaustible and eternal Beauty.

[6] Maritain On The Distinctive Realms of Philosophy and Theology, Nature and Grace.

Our treatment of the central theme of this book falls under the heading of "natural theology" according to the categories of classical Thomism. Once again, Jacques Maritain will clarify for us the distinction between this *natural theology* and what we usually mean when we use the term "theology" simply speaking: theology that proceeds from the foundation of Divinely revealed doctrine. From the point of departure of this distinction, wider realms of human intelligence can also be discerned. The order of the sciences that characterizes the intellect's approach to reality manifests clearly that religion is the summit of human existence (and indeed that the revealed religion of Christianity rests upon that summit).

Maritain presents the basic distinction between natural and revelation-based theology in his *Introduction to Philosophy*. Natural theology is the "knowledge of God which we can attain naturally by the unassisted powers of reason, and which enables us to know God by means of creatures as the origin of the natural order."[102] Revelation-based theology, however, enters into the realm of the *supernatural*; it involves a knowledge "unattainable naturally by the unassisted powers of reason, and is possible only if God has informed men about Himself by a revelation from which our reason, enlightened by faith, subsequently draws the implicit conclusions." The formal

---

[102] *An Introduction to Philosophy,* trans. E. I. Watkin (London and New York: Sheed and Ward, 1930 [original edition 1921]), p. 124. Hereafter cited as *Introduction*.

object of natural theology is "God as the first cause of creatures and the author of the natural order," whereas the formal object of supernatural theology is "God known in Himself, in His own divine life, or in technical language *sub ratione Deitatis.*"[103]

From this description, Maritain quickly extends his distinction to the whole order of philosophy (which reaches its summit in natural theology). The premises (naturally self-evident first principles) and the light (natural reason) of philosophy are independent of theology. Philosophy "develops its principles autonomously within its own sphere"—revelation is not an essential positive factor within the philosophical process, nor is it necessary in order to establish the foundations of philosophy. Theology exercises a "negative governance" over philosophy, since no philosophical formulation can contradict a theological truth. Theology can be said to exercise a positive regulation over philosophy only *per accidens*, insofar as it "turn[s] the investigations of philosophy in one direction rather than in another."[104]

Thus philosophy is "autonomous" in the constitutive characteristics it possesses as a discipline of the intellect. Of course, human reason itself is subordinate "in its very principles to the First Intellect." Moreover, philosophy is employed as an instrument within the theological process. Maritain views philosophy as instrumental to theology in three ways: (1) establishing the truths of fundamental theology [apologetics]; (2) providing analogous concepts that help illustrate in some measure the mysteries of faith;

---

103 *Introduction*, pp. 124-125.
104 *Introduction*, p. 127fn.

(3) refuting arguments constructed by human reason against the mysteries of faith [i.e. showing that the truths of faith do not contradict the exigencies of reason].[105]

In addition to this more precise relationship between philosophy and theology, Maritain notes the existential fecundity of these two realms of knowledge as they interact synergistically in the living experience of human knowing. In the mind of man, philosophy, by virtue of a vital contact with theology, is "superelevated" within its own order—existentially deepened in its capacity to perceive the truths which are proper to its own sphere. Moreover, when philosophy acts as an instrument of theology, it is enriched within itself, because "it is led to define more precisely and with more subtle refinements important concepts and theories, which, left to itself, it would be in danger of neglecting."[106]

Maritain is emphatic about excluding any *necessary* dependence of the intellect on the will in terms of its *per se* capacity to know metaphysical truth (which is not to deny that the will and other experiential factors may play a *de facto* psychological role in the complex journey of the human individual toward truth). Maritain's concern is to establish the objective character of conceptual knowledge and to distinguish himself from the theories of Maurice Blondel and his disciples. For this reason Maritain rejects the theory "that the first principles of being and the spiritual world are...disproportioned to the human intellect, not by defect, but by excess." Maritain understood the Blondelian assertion that the intellect by its very nature "is incapable of

---

[105] *Introduction*, pp. 130-131.
[106] *Introduction*, p. 131.

The Created Person and the Mystery of God

attaining [metaphysical truths] without the aid of love, of the will, of the virtues which rectify and control action" as an excessive importation of subjectivity into the realm of philosophy which ultimately compromised the mind's capacity to express the highest truths through the mediation of analogical *concepts.* Maritain's opposition to the Blondelian tendency in Christian philosophy rested on the same basis as his opposition to Bergsonism. Maritain's concern was that metaphysics—as an intellectual discipline—be capable of arriving at genuine conclusions and therefore holding a certain integrity within its own realm. Those Catholic philosophers in the early 1920s who insisted on the radical insufficiency of metaphysics ultimately failed to understand the proper role of analogy in the perception and expression of metaphysical principles and the subsequent development of metaphysics (and natural theology) as a genuine kind of knowledge: "these first principles of being are disproportioned to the *direct apprehension* of the intellect...Yet it can know them by analogy, in the mirror of the sensible..." It is, therefore, within the context of his defense of metaphysics as a genuine science that Maritain appears to oppose any *essential* role for affectivity and other psychological phenomena in the natural path toward *knowledge* about God and spiritual realities: "It remains that in the natural order, reason [in the realm of *metaphysics*] cannot have recourse to the will to acquire a knowledge of the absolute of which it would be [per se] incapable by itself."[107] As we have already noted, however, this does not mean that approaches

---

107 *Theonas: Conversations of a Sage,* trans. F. J. Sheed (London and New York: Sheed and Ward, 1933), pp. 179-180.

to God that rely on what we might call subjective "experiential" evidence have no value in the psychological order. What it does mean is that the scope of human reason in its journey toward God is not restricted to or *per se* dependent upon these experiential approaches. This is not to say, however, that such factors may not initiate, fructify, and invest with existential force the overall (subjective) personal conviction that someone has about God. These factors are the concrete resonance within the subject of what can be made cognitively explicit by metaphysics and natural theology.

Let us, however, continue to explore Maritain's overall insights on Thomistic epistemology as it stands by virtue of man's relationship to God. In the context of his critique of Descartes's sharp contrast between the "universal science" that brings all knowledge under the domain of human reason alone and a "faith" which is a (more or less) irrational affirmation of dogmas proposed by authority, Maritain clarifies further and develops his theory of the basic distinctions between the various intellectual "lights" of faith and contemplation, theology, and philosophy.

Faith, Maritain notes, "is an imperfect knowledge according to the mode of knowing (since it is founded wholly on the testimony of God, not on the evidence of the object itself)." Nevertheless, Maritain continues in line with the whole of the Thomistic tradition in saying that faith brings genuine knowledge: "a real knowledge, and superior to all human knowledge by its infallible certitude as well as by its object, which is God attained according to his own very essence."[108]

It is in the realm of supernatural knowing that Maritain begins to articulate his understanding of the interrelationship and continuity between distinct formal "lights" of knowledge. With regard to faith, Maritain insists—contrary to what he considered to be Descartes 'agnosticism' regarding intellectual penetration into the mysteries of revealed dogma—that the genuine and indeed superior knowledge given by faith, combined with its imperfection as a mode of knowing, instill within faith an intrinsic dynamism toward a more perfect way of grasping the truths it attains by its assent:

> By...faith it is given to us to enter into participation with the divine understanding, *intellegere divine*, and to consider all things as if with the eyes of God—*quasi oculo dei*. And so it tends toward evidence and being face to face with God as a movement tends toward its end...That is why the intellect, uplifted by faith to the divine truth, demands to be completed still further by the gifts of intelligence and wisdom..."[109]

---

[108] *The Dream of Descartes, Together With Some Other Essays*, trans. Mabelle L. Andison (New York: Philosophical Library, 1944), p. 64. Hereafter cited as *Dream*.

[109] *Dream*, p. 64.

Faith is therefore "a growing force, which in growing supernaturalizes the whole soul, and which has its full development only in the fully supernaturalized soul."[110]

The connection between faith and theology is founded upon a similar interpenetration of different ways of knowing. In the case of rational theology, however, the "growing force" of faith with its intrinsic urge to understand stimulates man's natural intellectual faculty to "seek understanding" according to its own method of analogous reasoning. In theology, however, the analogies are not drawn from created reality (as they are in metaphysics); rather they are the 'revealed analogies' that have been used by God to propose propositionally the articles of faith.

Rational theology does not penetrate beyond these analogies to a direct knowledge of the mysteries they signify. Rather it is led to a more profound and more secure understanding of truths grasped (as they are in metaphysics) by the indirect perception of analogy rather than the direct perception of properly signifying concepts. Theological understanding is more profound in the measure that the analogies it reasons upon include supernatural mysteries that cannot be attained by any natural metaphysical perception. It is also more *secure* by virtue of the higher certitude afforded by the grace of faith.

Maritain, however, does not rest content with the greater *certitude* of the conclusions of theological reasoning, which are drawn out of Divine revelation grasped with the supernatural certitude of faith. Maritain wants to avoid turning theology into a kind of 'higher metaphysics' in which the philosophical mind is merely presented with

---

[110] *Dream*, p. 66.

more *principles* (which happen to be supernaturally revealed) to reason upon. Rather, Maritain emphasizes also the penetration of faith in the reasoning process of theology itself. Rational theology is "theological" in its intellectual actualization and not only in its foundation. As an intellectual virtue, theology is "formally natural" but "radically and virtually" supernatural. The natural reasoning process that man uses in theology is "strengthened" from within, not only by the special certitude of faith, but also by a "superior penetration and superior power of discernment" which faith communicates intrinsically to the theological reasoning process without thereby turning it into a formally supernatural mode of knowing. Here Maritain is proposing his critically important notion which he will elsewhere call "superelevation"—the way that grace fertilizes formally natural realities within their own proper sphere.[111]

Now at first glance it must be admitted that it is somewhat ambiguous as to how the "superior certitude, superior penetration and superior power of discernment" which render theology a formally natural but radically supernatural reasoning process differ from the effects that the light of faith has on what Maritain will come to call

---

[111] In theology, according to St. Thomas, "reason illuminated by faith is also strengthened by it, if not with regard to its mode of procedure, which remains our natural discursive mode with all its imperfections, at least with regard to its superior certitude, to its superior penetration and the superior power of discernment for which it is indebted to the height of the supernaturally believed principles into which it resolves its conclusions" (*Dream*, p. 70). Theology is "a formally natural intellectual virtue" which is "nevertheless supernatural in its root, radicaliter et virtualiter" (*Dream*, p. 70). Once again, we refer the reader also to the section in *Degrees* on the "superanalogy" of faith (pp. 241-244).

"Christian philosophy." In his critique of Descartes, Maritain emphasizes that the inferiority of the lights of philosophy to the light of faith is a "vital subordination." As an example of this kind of subordination, he refers to "the kind of 'continuity' formed by the hierarchized degrees of pure spirits, illuminating one another, *per intuitum intellectus*" wherein "the lower angel illumined by the higher angel is strengthened within by him in his own intellectual light." He then claims that something analogous takes place in the human order—"a sort of spiritual union between specifically different *habitus* maintains an inferior *habitus* or virtue in contact with a superior *habitus* or virtue." The example of this that Maritain stresses, however, is that of the relationship between faith and philosophy. He says that "the faith *habitus* strengthens the philosophical *habitus* in its own proper philosophical order with regard to a certain truth demonstrable by reason alone...and makes it bring forth with more force, more perfection and more certitude its purely rational act of adhesion to the truth."[112]

As we examine Maritain's thought more closely, it does appear clear that there is in fact a distinction between the way he conceives the relationship between faith and philosophy and the way he conceives the role of faith within theology. When fully worked out it presents itself as a very subtle but very crucial distinction.

In the initial text of his essays on Descartes (which were originally all written during the 1920s), the primary role of faith for philosophical reason was to supplement its indigence and correct its errors (which were due in large

---

[112] *Dream*, pp. 86-87.

measure to the woundedness of the intellect due to original sin):

> "...in the state of nature fallen and redeemed, if indeed reason remain 'physically' capable of knowing with its strength alone every truth of the natural order, it is still not morally possible that without the help of revelation it should succeed in discovering and bringing together in their purity all these speculative and practical truths."[113]

However, in footnote 120, which was written later (at least 1931) for the publication of the compendium as a book, we find this very important description of Christian Philosophy:

> "It is not only through the proposing of objects (accessible in themselves to natural reason, but which in fact natural reason alone fails to grasp or impairs), it is also because it modifies the internal dynamism of the activities of the subject...and because it centers these activities above philosophy, that faith brings the philosophical *habitus* to a state of integrity which surpasses the power of the forces of reason alone."[114]

---

[113] *Dream*, p. 97.
[114] *Dream*, pp. 207-208.

The effect of faith on philosophy, then, is not the same as its role within theology. In theology, reason operates in a superior fashion, permeated as it were by faith in such a way that the root of the whole theological enterprise—the vital source from which it springs in its principles, reasoning, and conclusions—is supernatural. Theology cannot be theology, it cannot be a living knowledge, without the grace of God.[115]

Philosophy, however, seems to benefit from faith in a subtly different way. Faith corrects and clarifies the proper objects of philosophy, and also manifests for philosophy the fact that it does not constitute the highest wisdom, because it centers the person on a realm that is higher than philosophical wisdom. It is in this way that faith "modifies the internal dynamisms of the subject" in such a way that philosophy can be described as "Christian."

In the *Preface to Metaphysics*, Maritain further elucidates his understanding of the process of natural knowledge and how it bears upon its proper object, which is *being*. The natural intellectual perception of being has two distinct "stages":

---

[115] Even if this faith is "unformed"—i.e. even if the theologian is a sinner—it is still understood to be a supernatural gift from God that remains and that is ordered to the sinner's supernatural end.

(1) being as immediately attained by the rational process as soon as it begins to think: "being 'clothed' in the diverse natures apprehended by the senses."[116]
(2) being as object of metaphysics—disengaged and isolated in its pure intelligible value by abstraction from the sensible quiddity."[117]

Regarding stage one, we can make two further distinctions: the particularized being of the philosophy of nature and natural sciences and the general category of "being" arrived at by common sense.

"The knowledge of common sense is a natural and spontaneous growth, the product, so to speak, of rational instincts, and has not yet attained the level of Science."[118] Yet it has a universal scope.

> "Common sense is therefore, as it were, a rough sketch of metaphysics, a vigorous and unreflective sketch drawn by the natural motion and spontaneous instincts of reason. This is why common sense attains a certain though unscientific knowledge of God, human personality, free will, and so on."[119]

---

116 *A Preface to Metaphysics: Seven Lectures on Being* (New York and London: Sheed and Ward, 1939), p. 20. Hereafter cited as *Preface*.
117 *Preface*, p. 26.
118 *Preface*, p. 35.
119 *Preface*, p. 35.

Common sense "reasons about particular objects basing itself *implicitly* on the being they possess." Such reasoning thus enables common sense to arrive, in its informal and rudimentary manner, at the ontological relationship between particular things and the God who causes them: "From the consideration of these particular objects it rises to their First Cause." It must consider, at least *implicitly*, "the being in objects" in order to "rise to the first Cause of all being." However, common sense 'considers' being as such—metaphysical being—in an *entirely implicit* manner; "by itself common sense cannot disengage this notion of being and envisage it in it distinctive mystery." However, metaphysical being "is the hidden sinew of all that common sense knows of the things of the spirit."[120] Thus, although common sense does not produce a "scientific" (i.e. metaphysical) proof of God's existence, it can arrive at down-to-earth but also firm certitude about God—which it expresses in various ways—because its reasoning about finite objects takes place in the context of an implicit sense of being. This sense of *being* is real and decisive for common sense reasoning, but it is not conceptually disengaged from *beings*.

This raises an interesting—perhaps parenthetical—epistemological issue. Can one say that this implicit sense of being serves, according to an image much used by a particular school of twentieth century Thomism, as a *horizon* which is not yet consciously noticed, but which is the context within which particular things take their definition?

---

[120] *Preface*, p. 36.

Maritain's consideration of common sense reasoning raises some intriguing questions that he does not treat, but which are relevant to the natural knowledge of God as it is accounted for within Thomistic epistemology. Some might argue that Maritain's account of common sense reasoning indicates a "pre-grasp" of being (as *ens commune*) present in the intellective faculty and actualized in every act of knowledge (which would account for the intellect's objective orientation *toward being*). The idea of the *vorgriff*, of course, will forever be associated with the particular genius of Karl Rahner. One need not be a Rahnerian, however, in order to raise this possibility with regard to *ens commune*. The distinctiveness of Rahner's position is not only its proposal of a "vorgriff auf esse;" it is above all what is ultimately a *univocal* identification of the "esse" thus grasped with Transcendent Esse, God. This accounts for the particular characteristics of Rahner's epistemology and the unthematic, 'anonymous' approach to God that permeates all human knowing.[121] No one would suggest, however, that an *a-priori* "unthematic" pre-grasp of God at the foundations of knowledge could be incorporated into Maritain's system.[122]

Nevertheless, Maritain's notion of common sense might indicate a more modest account of what Rahner calls the "pre-grasp of being"—not in the sense of a pre-grasp of the Absolute Being, but in the sense of "being" as a

---

121 Rahner proposes his Thomistic "metaphysics of knowledge" in his seminal study *Spirit in the World* (original edition: *Geist in Welt* [Innsbruck, 1939]; trans. based on the 1957 edition by William Dych (Montreal: Palm Publishers, 1968).

122 A study comparing the epistemology of Rahner and that of Maritain would certainly be interesting.

transcendental analogously predicated of all things that the intellect perceives. In order to say that the *object* of the intellect is being, does there need to be something structural or innate to the intellect that corresponds to being and that governs, vivifies, and orients the intellectual process from the first moment that it is engaged by an object outside the mind? Could this be the intellectual light, the created participation in the Divine Light (which bears not *directly* on Divine Being, as Rahner would have it, but on that created being proportioned to the created intellect—so that analogical intellection is still required to move [indirectly] toward God)? Maritain never raises the issue in these terms, but some may be inclined to wonder whether this kind of a proposal might be congenial with his system.

The standard "Existential Thomist" reply—in its vigorous intent to avoid anything resembling an *a-priori* in knowledge—is that the intellect is simply ordered to reality according to its universal characteristics (which can be accounted for sufficiently by its structure as an *abstractive*, super-sensible faculty), so that it is not *intrinsically* entelichized by any originally luminous orientation toward being, but becomes so only *in act*, by virtue of the being that every intelligible object possesses; thus a notion of being impresses itself primarily albeit implicitly upon the mind as soon as it begins to know any thing.

And in fact, Maritain's consideration of the objective and subjective dimensions of the "intellectual light" seem to imply that his view leans in the Existential Thomist direction. This would mean that his view of common sense simply puts a specific emphasis on the illuminating activity of a subjective intellectual *habitus* that is engendered by the encounter with being. Human thought "sets out from being,

The Created Person and the Mystery of God

but from being as it is immediately apprehended when the mind first awakes in the sensible world. That is its starting point."[123]

If in fact the grasp of *ens commune* involves a kind of rudimentary *habitus* that "awakens" in an encounter with the sensible world, then Maritain's comments regarding the role of intellectual light in more specific forms of knowing would need to be considered as suggestive of his conception of common sense.

With regard to *science*, Maritain makes this distinction: the objective light is the degree of immateriality that determines "the characteristic mode of intellectual apprehension or eidetic visualization" under which the intellect grasps certain objects. "At the same time, proportionate to this objective light there is a subjective light perfecting the subjective activity of the intellect, by which the intellect itself is proportioned to a given object, fitted to apprehend it." This is the intellectual *habitus* "concerned with the production or effectuation of the act of knowing." Maritain notes, however, that the object grasped under its objective light is "prior, not in time but in ontological rank" to the *habitus* even though each is causally necessary to the other.[124] With regard to metaphysics he expresses it as follows:

> "It is this perception of being [under its objective light] that determines the first moment at which the *habitus* comes to birth, and it is by the operation of this same habit

---

123 *Preface*, pp. 48-49.
124 *Preface*, p. 50.

thus developed that the being which is the metaphysician's distinctive object is more and more clearly perceived."[125]

It could be argued that this at least implies that the objective light of being, not disengaged in itself but shining within the intelligibility of a particular reality encountered by the senses, 'determines the first moment at which the *habitus* or quasi-*habitus* of common sense comes to birth.' Thus, Maritain would appear to be an *a-posteriorist*, insofar as he seems to indicate that *esse* only enters upon the horizon of knowing when it is (radically) introduced into human consciousness by means of a sense encounter and intelligible apprehension of an *ens*. However, Maritain does assign an important role to the power of implicit and explicit (but "pre-scientific") perception that takes place under the habitual light of common sense. Common sense's attainment of being—"veiled" though it may be—plays a crucial role in the progress and development of all knowledge, and in particular of metaphysics.

It is here, in the *Preface to Metaphysics,* that Maritain develops in particular his distinctive theory of the decisive insight that constitutes metaphysics as a genuine knowledge: the "intuition of being." For Maritain the birth of the intellect into the realm of the metaphysical is analogous to its first taste of knowledge; indeed the intuition of being is rooted in the intuition of common sense, but it achieves full and explicit understanding of its own content. Here it is important to note that Maritain distinguishes the term *intuition of being,* as the distinctly

---

[125] *Preface*, p. 50.

explicit metaphysical intuition, from the initial intuition implicitly attained by all knowledge, the *intuition of common sense*. Maritain will sometimes use the former term in a broad sense to indicate both types of intuition, even while he clearly distinguishes their content. "It is being which the intellect perceives first and before anything else. It is, therefore, being which the metaphysical intellect must disengage and know in its distinctive mystery."[126] Indeed, Maritain emphasizes that "the assurance which underlies the entire process of thought...belongs, in fact, *to the obscure intuition of being possessed by the common sense*."[127] In the metaphysical intuition of being, this assurance is "confirmed, strengthened, and made self-conscious."[128]

Maritain is inclined to classify the intuition of being not as an achievement of intellectual concentration, but rather as a kind of "natural revelation to the soul"—a "gift bestowed upon the intellect" which can even resemble at times (analogously, and on a natural level) a mystical grace.[129]

Here is where Maritain attempts to give "metaphors, lamentably inadequate" for the intuition of being as it is experienced:

> "What is now perceived is, as it were, a pure activity, a subsistence, but a subsistence which transcends the entire order of the

---

[126] *Preface*, p. 59.
[127] *Preface*, p. 66.
[128] *Preface*, p. 63 (footnote).
[129] *Preface*, p. 52.

imaginable, a living tenacity, at once precarious—it is nothing for me to crush a fly—and indomitable—within and around me there is growth without ceasing. By this subsistence, this tenacity, objects come up against me, overcome possible disaster, endure, and possess in themselves whatever is requisite for this."[130]

Some modern existentialist philosophers (e.g. Gabriel Marcel) reject the intellectual character of metaphysics because they presuppose the idealist conception of intellect. "In consequence of this prejudice," the existentialist of this type "will seek to make contact with the ontological mystery, so to speak, by a circuitous route which leads through the subjective domain, therefore specifically by way of the obscure apprehension of love." Such existentialists are skeptical about intellectualist metaphysics, and seek instead to attain an experience of the heart of reality that is not blocked by a constraining and (it seems) necessarily falsifying *idea* of being. But Maritain insists that it is not the *idea* of being which is the object of metaphysical *scientia*; it is being itself. The attractiveness of existentialist analysis as an alternative to rationalism in the end depends on this fact. For the "obscure apprehension of love" really does "enter [being] after its fashion, as does intellect after its own."[131]

This reflection on the intellectual intuition of being and on the manner in which love also penetrates the mystery of

---

[130] *Preface*, pp. 56-57.

[131] *Preface*, p. 63 (footnote).

The Created Person and the Mystery of God

being ("after its fashion"—and we might add according to the transcendental feature of being which is "the good") prompts Maritain to venture some remarkable reflections on the proper metaphysical character of knowledge and love.

He classifies knowledge and love as the "overflow" of spiritual being, and places this classification within the wider context of a feature that is characteristic of all beings. Every being has a natural appetite, an intrinsic superabundance, "a tendency to expand and pass beyond itself, to communicate a surplus" either through transitive action which perfects another or through immanent organic development by which its own being is increased. "Th[e] acquisition of a new perfection accompanies in every creature the superabundance of which I am speaking. But it is not *of itself*...implied by it. Formally it is the superabundance as such which is essential."[132] In the case of God, the superabundant "overflow of intellection and love which constitutes His Being itself" does not bring about any *increase* in His perfection. For the spiritual creature, this inherent ontological expansiveness realizes itself in "a superabundance of a higher order" than that which characterizes physical beings, a "supra-subjective existence...of the intentional order" which Maritain terms "existence as a gift."[133]

---

[132] *Preface*, pp. 72-73.

[133] *Preface*, p. 73. Elsewhere Maritain comments on the orientation proper to spiritual being, and sees it properly fulfilled in the order of grace: "All things (like intelligence and art) that touch the transcendental order and consequently find themselves realized in the pure state in God and 'by participation' in created subjects" experience "an antinomy...between the highest demands of the *essence* taken in itself and transcendentally, and the *conditions of existence* called for by this very essence according as it is realized here on earth...In the very measure in which they tend (with a

The fact that truth is a transcendental, analogously predicable of every being, means that "transparence to mind, communicability, is co-extensive with being. To the extent to which anything is, it is transparent, communicable, it possesses a certain measure of communicability, a diffusiveness, a generosity."[134]

Correspondingly, the nature of *esse* as a super-abundant act which is the root of a thing's movement toward perfection constitutes the metaphysical basis for the principle of finality: "*Being is love of good, every being is the love of a good*, and this love is the very ground of its action."[135] Every being has an innate tendency to the ecstasy

---

tendency that is inefficacious, but nonetheless real) to the fullness of their essence *considered in itself* (transcendentally) *and in its pure formal line*, they tend to go beyond themselves, to exceed the limits of their essence *considered in a created subject* (with the specific determinations which belong to it there), and at the same stroke to escape from their *conditions of existence*." This tendency toward the transcendental perfection of a creaturely participated essence is, it seems, the basic dynamism underlying both great sin and great holiness (with the difference depending on whether or not creaturehood and its corresponding existential dependence are acknowledged and embraced even within the transcendental movement). Thus the intellect in man, "in whom it is *reason*," aspires toward the superhuman reality of intellection as such—aspires "to go beyond both the limits as reason and its conditions of existence in the [human] subject." This aspiration pursues one of two paths: either 'grace...intervene[s] to superelevate nature" and man, by cooperating with this grace, is transfigured by the *gifts* of faith and infused contemplation; or man succumbs to "the angelist swoon...into a 'pure intellection' which is then a mystical suicide of thought." See The Frontiers of Poetry, pp. 122-123 and footnote 178 on p.224. This certainly relates to our discussion above of the "trans-natural desire."

134 *Preface*, p. 80.
135 *Preface*, p. 110.

The Created Person and the Mystery of God

of goodness, a tendency "to impart to itself or another a perfection, a surplus."[136]

Thus every being, in so far as it is a being, is an agent. 'Being toward' is in fact not the prerogative of man (as Heidegger thought); it is inherent to the dynamic character of *esse* itself. "Being as agent is *reference to and determination to* a particular good, is appetite, tendency, desire, an urge, toward a surplus, a superabundance, a glory."[137] Note that for Maritain the effusive superabundance of being is termed "glory." It would be interesting to explore further the ramifications that this has for Maritain's aesthetics.

Note also how Maritain identifies *intentional being*: "the being...in virtue of which a being is more than itself, exists over and above its own existence."[138]

Everything that is, is a tendency to the good which is its particular operation. Maritain refers to a scholastic formula: *Omnis res est propter suam operationem*; everything exists *for its operation*. Does this mean that substance (the thing) exists for the sake of accident (an operation)? Maritain paraphrases Cajetan's answer as follows: "Everything exists for itself in an operation, for inasmuch as it is in operation, it attains its ultimate actuality."[139]

Thus we can conclude that for Maritain, the realization of knowledge and love constitute for man the fulfillment of his being, his "ultimate actuality." In this intentionality,

---

136 *Preface*, p. 111.
137 *Preface*, p. 110.
138 *Preface*, pp. 109-110.
139 *Preface*, p. 120.

man exists beyond himself, which implies—it seems—*beyond his nature*, at least in the etymological sense of nature as that which is given at the origin of a thing. In this sense, indeed, all things transcend their 'original structure' in the measure in which they *realize* the finality toward which they are oriented by nature. What must be understood in greater detail is how this "super-existence" in which man knows God analogously via metaphysics, and loves God as origin of his being and highest object of his intellectual nature, is distinguished from the "super-existence" of knowledge and love that man achieves by means of revelation and faith, charity and contemplative wisdom, and—finally—the beatific vision itself. As Maritain says:

> "In view of the relationship in which creatures stand to God, the affirmation that God should not only be loved but that He loves, I mean with the distinctive *madness* of love, and that there can be relations of friendship, mutual self-giving, community of life, and the sharing of a common bliss between God and His creatures, implies the supernatural order of grace and charity."[140]

Maritain's metaphysics takes us ultimately to something greater than the "metaphysics of knowledge." It is *being itself* that is the object of metaphysics, and thus the realist metaphysician comes to know that he *is* something much more profound than just a self-enclosed intellect with an

---

[140] *Preface*, p. 95.

idea of being. And with this, the enclosure that traps being within itself is broken down and we find ourselves in a universe of *communion*, a universe in which every being attains its fullness by becoming a *gift*. In this context, the metaphysical character of a being as a *sign* becomes more coherent. It is intrinsic to every being to go beyond itself and "indicate" its Goal, the Fullness after which it was patterned. Thus beings are signs not only because they reflect their origin, but also because of the active dynamism of their orientation toward their specific "ends," an orientation which consists in a self-diffusive "manifesting" of the Transcendent Good. If in the hierarchy of the universe things are "for the sake of" persons, then it is not unreasonable to conclude that this manifestation on the part of sub-rational beings is a kind of *communication* that illuminates and orients personal beings in the unfolding of their dynamism of knowing and loving. And, *a fortiori*, this would apply to relationships between persons.

Everything is true, good, and beautiful, and therefore everything is self-diffusive. It is in the person that this ontological "gift-character" of existence becomes aware of itself and, from the foundation of knowledge and self-possession, gives himself in freedom to the One who possesses and governs all things.

Part III: A Complementary Approach: Outline of the Existential Religious Philosophy of Luigi Giussani

Luigi Giussani, who has been frequently cited in Part I of this text, has made a significant contribution to Catholic philosophy and theology.[142] In this segment we want to give a brief outline of the central thesis of the book by Giussani that has recently been published in a scholarly edition in English, entitled *The Religious Sense*.[143] Here, we hope, it will become clear that Giussani's thought presents a profound theological analysis of human "psychology" (in the classical sense of this term); indeed it represents a tremendous resource toward the development of a fully adequate Catholic theological anthropology and philosophy of religion.

Giussani proposes what he calls "the religious sense" as the foundation of the human person's awareness of himself and his concrete engagement of life. The term "religious sense" does not imply that Giussani thinks that man's need for religion is part of the organic structure of his bodily senses, nor does he mean that religion is to be defined as a mere emotional sensibility or a vague kind of feeling. Rather, Giussani uses the term "sense" here in the same way that we refer to "common sense" or the way that John Henry Newman sought to identify what he called the

---

[142] Two large volumes of Giussani's *Opere* published by Jaca Book in Milan in 1992 include not only *Il Senso Religioso* and its companion volumes, but also significant treatises on subjects as diverse as educational theory, the liturgy, the Christian dimension of morality, and even a study of twentieth century Protestant theologians in America. In the past ten years, Giussani has been published extensively, above all in books compiled from retreat conferences that are notable for their theological as well as pastoral richness.

[143] *The Religious Sense*, trans. John Zucchi (Montreal & Kingston: McGill-Queen's University Press, 1997)

"illative sense." "Sense" refers to a dynamic spiritual process within man; an approach to reality in which man's *intelligence* is fully engaged, but not according to those categories of formal analysis that we call "scientific." Giussani's understanding of the "religious sense" in man has a certain kinship to Jacques Maritain's view that man can come to a "pre-philosophical" or "pre-scientific" awareness of the existence of God, in that both positions insist that reason is profoundly involved in the approach to God for every human being—not just for philosophers.[144] What is distinctive about Giussani's approach, however, is his effort to present a descriptive analysis of the very core of reason, the wellspring from which the human person, through action, enters into relationship with reality. Needless to say, "action" in the Giussanian sense is not simply to be identified with an external "activism," but involves also and primarily what Maritain would call the *supremely vital act* by which man seeks to behold and embrace truth, goodness, and beauty—those interrelated transcendental perfections inherent in all things which Giussani refers to by a disarmingly simple term: *meaning*.

Giussani proposes that we observe ourselves "in action"—that we investigate seriously the fundamental dispositions and expectations that shape the way we approach every circumstance in life. In so doing, we will discover that the "motor" that generates our activity and places us in front of things with a real interest in them is something within ourselves that is both reasonable and mysterious. It is something so clear and obvious that a child can name it, and yet it is something so mysterious that

---

[144] See Jacques Maritain, *Approaches to God*, pp. 1-15.

no one can really define what it is: it is the search for *happiness*. The human heart—that is, "heart" in the biblical sense, as the center of the person, the foundation of intelligence and freedom and not merely the seat of infrarational emotions and sentiments—the human heart seeks happiness in all of its actions. Here of course Giussani is saying the same thing as St. Thomas Aquinas. Giussani opens up new vistas on this classical position, however, by engaging in an existentially attentive analysis of the characteristics of this "search." Giussani emphasizes the dramatic, arduous, and mysterious character of the need for happiness as man actually experiences it. He says that if we really analyze our desires and expectations—even in the most ordinary and mundane circumstances—what we will find is not some kind of desire for happiness that we can easily obtain, package, and possess through our activity. Rather we will see that genuine human action aims at "happiness" by being the enacted expression of certain fundamental, mysterious, and seemingly open-ended *questions*. The heart, the self, when acting—when the person is working, playing, eating, drinking, rising in the morning, or dying—is full of the desire for something and the search for something that it does not possess, that it cannot give to itself, and that it does not even fully understand, although the heart is aware that this Object is *there*, and its attainment is a real possibility.

Giussani claims that religiosity coincides with these fundamental questions:

> The religious factor represents the nature of our "I" in as much as it expresses itself in certain questions: "What is the ultimate meaning of existence?" or "Why is there pain

and death, and why, in the end, is life worth living?" Or, from another point of view: "What does reality consist of and what is it made for?" Thus, the religious sense lies within the reality of our self at the level of these questions.[145]

This means that, according to Giussani, man becomes authentically religious to the extent that he develops and articulates in the face of the circumstances of life the basic natural complex of questions or "needs" that are identified in the first chapter of the book as *constitutive* of the human heart: the need for truth, justice, goodness, happiness, beauty.[146] This complex of "needs" which constitutes the human heart by nature, will become more and more explicit and urgent as the person lives life and pursues the things that attract him, if he is truly honest with himself.

Man wants happiness by nature. I want happiness. So I go out and buy a car. The car gives me a taste of happiness but does not fully satisfy the desire. So my desire becomes a question: "What will make me truly and fully happy?" Or perhaps after I have bought that car and I am still enjoying the taste of partial happiness that it gives me, I get into an accident and wreck my beautiful new possession. My simple desire finds itself full of questions: "Why was I not able to hold onto that thing and the satisfaction it gave me? Why do I lose things? Why is life so fragile, and is there something that won't let me down?"

---

[145] *The Religious Sense*, p. 45.

[146] *The Religious Sense*, see pp. 7-10.

The Created Person and the Mystery of God

The more we take our own selves and our actions seriously, the more we perceive the mysteriousness and also the urgency of these questions, the fact that *we cannot really avoid them*; they are necessarily at the root of everything we do. This is because it is the nature of the human being to expect something, to look for fulfillment in everything he does. And where is the limit to this desire to be fulfilled? There is no limit. It is un-limited. Every achievement, every possession opens up on a further possibility, a depth that remains to be explored, a sense of incompleteness, a yearning for more. We are like hikers in the mountains (an analogy Giussani is fond of): we see a peak and we climb to the top. When we arrive there, we have a new view, and in the distance we see a higher peak promising a still greater vista.

Giussani quotes the great 19th century Italian poet Giacomo Leopardi—who is speaking here in the persona of a shepherd watching his flock by night, conversing with the moon:[147]

> And when I gaze upon you,
> Who mutely stand above the desert plains
> Which heaven with its far circle but confines,
> Or often, when I see you
> Following step by step my flock and me,
> Or watch the stars that shine there in the sky,
> Musing, I say within me:
> "Wherefore those many lights,
> That boundless atmosphere,
> And infinite calm sky? And what the meaning

---

[147] *The Religious Sense*, p. 46.

Of this vast solitude? And what am I?

There are a couple of points about this striking poetic excerpt that are worth mentioning as illustrative of central themes in Giussani. The first point is this: note that the shepherd's questions are so poignantly expressed "from the heart" (*Musing, I say within me*). They are "personal" questions we might say; that is, they are questions that seem deeply important to the shepherd's own life, that emerge from the shepherd's solitude as he watches the flocks by night and gazes at the moon. And yet, the questions themselves are really "philosophical" questions: "metaphysical" questions which ask about the relationship of the universe to its mysterious Source, and "anthropological" questions about the nature of the world, of man, of the self. Let us note these things only to emphasize that Giussani's evaluation of the dynamic of the human heart is not exclusively concerned with the pursuit of external objects and the way in which these objects lead "beyond" themselves the acting person who engages them. Giussani stresses that the *need for truth* is inscribed on the human heart; the need to see the meaning of things is fundamental to man. Hence the "objectivity" required for addressing philosophical and scientific questions does not imply that these questions are detached from the "heart" of the person who deals with them. When the scientist scans that infinite, calm sky and that vast solitude with his telescope, he must record what he sees—not what he wishes he would have seen. In this sense he must be "objective," and his questions and methodology must be detached from his own particular interests. But what puts him behind that telescope in the first place is his own personal need for truth, and this need grows and articulates itself more and more as questions emerge in the light of his discoveries. All of this could be applied by analogy to the researches carried out by a true philosopher.

The second point is this: Leopardi's poem conveys with imaginative force the inexhaustibility of the human desire and the questions through which it is expressed, or at least tends to be expressed insofar as man is willing to live in a way that is true to himself (several chapters of Giussani's book are devoted to the various ways in which man is capable of distracting himself or ignoring the dynamic of the religious sense, or anesthetizing himself against its felt urgency). Even more importantly, he indicates that the unlimited character of man's most fundamental questions points toward an Infinite Mystery, a mystery that man continually stands in front of with fascination and existential hunger, but also with *questions*, because he is ultimately unable by his own power to unveil its secrets.

The experience of life teaches man, if he is willing to pay attention to it, that what he is truly seeking—in every circumstance—is the unfathomable mystery which alone corresponds to the depths of his soul.[148] Offer to man

---

[148] St. Thomas Aquinas, in fact, brilliantly and concisely expresses the metaphysical foundations that underlie Giussani's penetrating psychological analysis of man's "religious sense." In Question 22, art. 2 of *De Veritate*, St. Thomas affirms that not only man, but all creatures in a certain sense "naturally tend to God implicitly" even if they do not have the capability of doing so explicitly. This is because every creature, in pursuing the created good corresponding to its own nature and capacities, is ultimately ordained to God as primary end just as every creature comes forth into being and operates as a 'secondary efficient cause' by virtue of God's primary causality. Every "secondary end is sought only by reason of the worth of the principal end existing in it inasmuch as it is subordinated to the principal

anything less than the Infinite and you will frustrate him, whether he admits it or not. Yet at the same time man is not able to grasp the Infinite by his own power. Man's power is limited, and anything it attains it finitizes, it reduces to the measure of itself. The desire of man as a person, however, is unlimited, which means that man does not have the power to completely satisfy himself; anything that he makes is going to be *less* than the Infinite.

Here we begin to see clearly why Giussani holds that the ultimate questions regarding the meaning, the value, and the purpose of life have a religious character; and how it is that these questions are asked by everyone within the ordinary, non-theoretical reasoning process which he terms "the religious sense." The human heart is—in fact—a great, burning question, a plea, an insatiable hunger, a fascination and a desire for the unfathomable mystery that underlies

end or has its likeness. Accordingly, because God is the last end, He is sought in every end, just as, because He is the first efficient cause, He acts in every agent." Thus St. Thomas concludes that all things seek God at least implicitly. But, as Giussani points out, man is "that level of nature wherein nature becomes aware of itself and of its own purposes" and it is precisely by means of the unfolding of the religious sense that man becomes aware of the fact that he and all things are made for God. St. Thomas explains the same point as follows: He notes that "nothing has the note of appetibility except by a likeness to the first goodness"—this means that every created end is a 'secondary end' that *appeals* only insofar as it reflects a dimension of the inexhaustible desireableness of the Primary Good. However "only a rational nature can trace secondary ends back to God by a sort of analytic procedure so as to seek God Himself explicitly. In demonstrative sciences a conclusion is correctly drawn only by a reduction to first principles. In the same way the appetite of a rational creature is correctly directed only by an explicit appetitive tendency to God either actual or habitual." St. Thomas's reference to "trac[ing] secondary ends back to God *by a sort of analytic procedure*" indicates precisely the kind of analysis that Giussani is encouraging contemporary man to undertake.

reality and that gives life its meaning and value. This mystery is something Other than any of the limited things that we can perceive or produce; indeed it is their fundamental Source. Therefore the all-encompassing and limitless search that constitutes the human heart and shapes our approach to everything is a *religious* search. It is indeed, as we shall see in a moment, a search for "God."

Man seeks an infinite fulfillment, an infinite coherence, an infinite interpenetration of unity between persons, an infinite wisdom and comprehension, an infinite love, an infinite perfection. Yet man does not have the capacity to achieve any of these things by his own power. Yet, in spite of this incapacity, in spite of the fact that the mystery of life—the mystery of happiness—seems always one step beyond us, our natural inclination is *not* one of despair, but rather one of dogged persistence and constant hope. Giussani insists that this hope and expectation is what most profoundly shapes the self; when I say the word "I," I express this center of hope and expectation of infinite perfection and happiness that is coextensive with myself, that "is" myself, my *heart*. And when I say the word "you," truly and with love, then I am acknowledging that same undying hope that shapes your self.

The human person walks on the roads of life with his hands outstretched toward the mystery of existence, constantly pleading for the fulfillment he seeks—not in despair but with hope—because the circumstances and events of life contain a promise, they whisper continually that happiness is possible. This is what gives the human spirit the strength to carry on even in the midst of the greatest difficulties.

Let us note two further points. First of all: I cannot answer the ultimate questions about the meaning of my life, and yet every fiber of my being seeks that answer and expects it. There must be Another who does correspond to my heart, who can fill the need that I *am*. To deny the possibility of an answer is to uproot the very foundation of the human being and to render everything meaningless. As Macbeth says, it would be as if life is "a tale told by an idiot, full of sound and fury, signifying nothing."[149] There *must* be an answer; and a human being cannot live without seeking that answer. Giussani says that a human being cannot live five minutes without affirming something—consciously or unconsciously—that makes those five minutes *worthwhile*.[150] This is the basic structure of human reason at its root. "Just as an eye, upon opening, discovers shapes and colors, so human reason—by engaging the problems and interests of life—seeks and affirms some ultimate" value and significance which gives meaning to everything."[151] But if we are honest, if we realize that we cannot fulfill ourselves, if we face the fact that the answer to the question of the meaning of life is not something we can discover among our possessions, or measure or dominate or make with our own hands, then we begin to recognize that our need for happiness points to Someone Else, to an Infinite Someone who alone can *give us* what we seek.

Second: This longing of my heart, this seeking of the Infinite is not something I made up or chose for myself. It

---

[149] Macbeth, act V., scene V.
[150] *The Religious Sense*, p. 57
[151] *The Religious Sense*, p. 58

is not my idea or my project or my particular quirk. It corresponds to the way I am, to the way I "find myself" independent of any of my personal preferences or decisions. It is at the root of me. It is at the root of every person. It is in fact *given* to me, and to every person—this desire for the Mystery that is at the origin of everything that I am and do. In the depths of my own self there is this hidden, insatiable hunger and thirst, this "heart that says of You, 'seek His face!'" (Psalm 27:8), this need for an Other that suggests His presence at the origin of my being. He gives me my being; He is "nearer to me than I am to myself" as St. Augustine says. And He has made me *for Himself*; He has placed within each of us a desire that goes through all the world in search of signs of His presence. In the depths of our being, we are not alone. We are made by Another and for Another. "You have made us for Yourself, O Lord, and our hearts are restless until they rest in You," says St. Augustine.

Thus Giussani teaches that the Mystery of God is the only reality that corresponds to the "heart" of man: to the fundamental questions of human reason and the fundamental desire of human freedom. It is this Infinite Mystery that the human person seeks in every circumstance of life. In our work, our loves, our friendships, our leisure time, our eating and drinking, our living and dying—in all of these activities we seek the face of the unfathomable Mystery that we refer to with poor words like "happiness" or "fulfillment" or "perfection."

St. Thomas Aquinas says that God is happiness by His Essence, and we are called to participate in His happiness by being united to Him who is Infinite Goodness[152] We are made for happiness. By our very nature we seek happiness. To be religious, then, is to recognize that God alone can make us happy. It is to recognize the mysterious *existential reflection* of God's infinite truth, goodness, and beauty that radiates from every creature, that lights up the circumstances of our lives, and calls out to us through all the opportunities that life presents to us.

In this sketch of Giussani's understanding of what he calls "the religious sense," we can see that religion cannot be relegated to the fringes of life. Religion is not to be simply delineated as one aspect of life: a comfort for our sentiments, a list of ethical rules, a foundation for the stability of human social life (even though it entails such things as various consequences that follow from what it is in itself). Rather, the realm of the religious is coextensive with our happiness. The proper position of the human being is to live each moment *asking* for God to give him the happiness he seeks but cannot attain by his own power. *Asking for true happiness*—this is the true position of man in front of everything. Giussani often points out that— "structurally" (that is, by nature)—man is a "beggar" in front of the mystery of Being.

This brings us to the final chapters of *The Religious Sense*, in which Giussani analyses the dramatic character of this truth about man, both in terms of the very nature of this position of "being a beggar" and in terms of how this truth has played itself out in the great drama of human history. We could all too easily allow ourselves to be lulled to sleep by all of this lovely language about desiring the Infinite

---

152 *Summa Theologiae* I-II, q. 3, a. 1, reply ob. 1

The Created Person and the Mystery of God

Mystery, and end up missing the point. The image of the beggar ought not to be romanticized in our imaginations. Generally people don't like to be beggars, and they don't have much respect for beggars. We should be able to attain what we need by our own efforts; is this not a basic aspect of man's sense of his own dignity? And yet the very thing we need most is something that we do not have the power to attain, something we must *beg for*. This is the true human position, and yet it is not as easy to swallow as it may first appear to be.

We are beggars in front of our own destiny because the Infinite One for whom our hearts have been made is always beyond the things of this world that point toward Him but do not allow us to extract His fullness from them by our own power. This fact causes a great tension in the experience of the human person—a "vertigo," a dizziness, Giussani calls it[153]—and there results the inevitable temptation to shrink the scope of our destiny, to attempt to be satisfied with something within our power, something we are capable of controlling and manipulating. This, says Giussani, is the essence of *idolatry*. Instead of allowing ourselves to be "aimed" by the beauty of things toward a position of poverty and begging in front of *the* Beauty who is "ever beyond" them, the Mystery of Infinite Splendor who sustains them all—who holds them in the palm of his hand—we try instead to grasp these finite things and make them the answer to our need for the Infinite.

This great tension at the heart of man's religious sense—and the historical tragedy of man's failure to live truly according to the religious sense—generates within the heart

---

153 *The Religious Sense*, p. 135.

of man the longing for *salvation*. Corresponding to this longing, Giussani says, is the recognition of the *possibility of revelation*. Might not the Infinite Mystery make Himself manifest in history, create a way within history for me to reach Him? Might not the Infinite Mystery who constitutes my happiness approach me, condescend to my weakness, guide my steps toward Him? This possibility—the possibility of Divine Revelation—is profoundly "congenial" to the human person, because man feels profoundly his need for "help" in achieving his mysterious destiny.

Thus *The Religious Sense* concludes on this note: the possibility of revelation. Here the ground is laid for the second book in what might be called Giussani's catechesis of Christian anthropology: *The Origin of the Christian Claim*. In this book, Giussani will propose that Christ is the revelation of God in history, the Mystery drawn close to my life, walking alongside the human person. Christ is the great Divine *help* to the human person on the path to true happiness. In the third book *Why The Church*, he discusses how Christ is to be encountered concretely today in the Church.

We are at a transition point in our analysis. Having viewed the essentially religious character of human existence from a variety of viewpoints, we will now turn, in the concluding Part IV, to some points regarding the religion which God in His mercy has given to man, the religion that transforms man and in so doing does eminent justice to his humanity: the religion of Jesus Christ.

Part IV: Jesus Christ Preached by the Church: Some Suggestions Toward the Solution of the Problem of Man

[1] Jesus

As we have already noted, it is not the purpose of this book to give an apologetical treatment of the claim of Christianity to be the revelation of God (although we have frankly admitted that we do indeed believe that it is). Rather, we are trying to identify the human context (which, as we have seen, means the *religious* context) within which this claim presents itself. It is necessary, nonetheless, for us to approach the figure of Jesus of Nazareth, who is indeed the historical man who has so powerfully shaped and provoked this human context.

Modern, "post-Christian" rationalists still like to assert that Jesus was not God, but merely a great man. In so doing, however, they find themselves in a strange dilemma. On the one hand, anthropocentric rationalism or positivism must reject the incarnation, because they reject a-priori the possibility of the supernatural, and therefore the possibility that God could reveal himself in a mode that transcends human scientific reason or perception. The Christian doctrine of the incarnation—as the most profound kind of supernatural revelation—therefore simply cannot be true. It is the business of apologetics (which we will not engage in here) to show that—in spite of all the pseudoscholarly historical evasions put forth during the past 300 years—a serious treatment of the gospels and the milieu of early Christianity reveals clearly that the man Jesus of Nazareth claimed to be God. Now, on the one hand already mentioned, modernism cannot admit the possibility that Jesus's claim could be true. On the other hand, however, the secular mentality is not willing to follow all the way to the end the logic of rejecting this claim—it refuses to say that Jesus was a madman, a religious charlatan, a colossal megalomaniac. The Jesus who is portrayed in the gospels acts with the authority of God and demands the reverence due to God. And it is an historical fact that the earliest Christians gave him that reverence, to the point of sacrificing their lives. If Jesus was not God, the best thing that we can say about him is that he was a madman. If he were knowingly *pretending* to be God, then we must condemn him as a criminal and a deceiver, indeed history's most destructive cult leader. But the majority of people don't want to draw this conclusion, because the evidence is so strong that Jesus was *not* a madman, much less an evil man; rather, many are still willing to grant that he was the greatest man who ever lived on the face of the earth.[154] Why is this? The problem is that our secularized culture wants to deny the divinity of Christ *but at the same time keep His humanity*. And this, indeed, is part of a larger problem with the agenda of the post-Christian Western world: It wants to deny the supernatural while holding onto that magnificent consequence of the supernatural—the "new humanity" that it generates, the human goodness and nobility that has entered the world only because God entered the world. We want the human fruits of Christianity without its Divine, supernatural roots; we want the branches without the Vine. But as our culture proves more and more every day, *when the branch is cut off from the vine it withers away.*

---

[154] Of course, this basic observation is one of the crucial points of contemporary apologetics, in the arguments of C.S. Lewis, G.K. Chesterton, and others.

Perhaps, however, there is something hopeful about the fact that the ideological stance of our culture prefers to maintain this contradictory interpretation of Jesus (though, in the post-modern world, admiration for the [merely] human figure of Jesus is increasingly giving way to appalling ignorance about Him). At least something of Jesus has remained in the awareness of people (dead branches drying up on the ground still belong to the vine, and as St. Paul tells us they can be grafted back on). In any case, the reluctance of our culture to "let go" completely of Jesus is understandable. The figure of Jesus constantly fascinates anyone who looks at Him with any degree of seriousness. It requires a completely vitiated human heart to read the gospels and not be somehow moved by that man, moved to say, "He is good, extraordinarily good."

Let us therefore consider some of the facets of Jesus's goodness as a man, His human greatness, His sublime beauty. Indeed, the utter singularity of Jesus as a human figure is clear from everything we know about Him. In the humanity of Jesus that the gospels portray, we see all the attractiveness of life, all the tenderness and depth and value of the human condition shining forth and commanding our interest and affection.[155] We can see this in the consideration of His attributes, both the simple ones and the

---

155 Hans Urs Von Balthasar comments on the "incontrovertible unified effect of the intact figure of Jesus" that shines through in the Gospels in spite of particular difficulties that exegetes try to raise. Von Balthasar emphasizes the compelling nature of the "whole Jesus" who emerges as a single integral figure of unique splendor who coheres as a person in all the Gospel accounts. Von Balthasar ought not, however, to reject the rational value of classical apologetics. See "Does Jesus Shine Through?" in *New Elucidations*, trans. Sr. Mary Theresilde Skerry (San Francisco: Ignatius, 1986).

outstanding ones. For pedagogy's sake, let us attempt a schematic classification:

(1) JESUS IS A REALIST. The gospels show us that Jesus of Nazareth is a man of intense awareness and focus. He has an unequaled familiarity and sympathy for the world and for those tiny details in the lives of people that unveil their souls. Almost every page of the gospels reveals the interest Jesus has in everything around Him. He notices things, even small things, in a deeply human way. The stories that make up so much of Jesus's teaching are full of the stuff of ordinary life, the particulars of His environment. Jesus speaks about farmers and businessmen, crafty servants, children in the marketplace, fathers and sons, fig trees whose buds signal the beginning of summer, the old widow who lights a lamp and sweeps the house looking for her lost coin, "Herod the fox". But Jesus's attitude is much more than just a poetic sense of irony and metaphor. It is rooted in a clear-eyed and penetrating attention to the real world, a remarkable capacity for judgment, a genius for sizing up situations and persons. Jesus engages the concrete details of life; He is a man who sees the world as it is.

(2) JESUS IS A MAN OF GREAT EMOTIONAL RESPONSIVENESS. "I have come to cast fire on the earth!" Jesus is (in the best sense of the term) a passionate man. He feels the whole range of human emotions, in a way that energizes His human responsiveness in every situation. He feels outrage and indignation at the hypocrisy of the powerful men of His time. He drives the buyers and sellers out of the temple with a whip of cords. Yet He is also a man of magnificent tenderness, "moved with pity" by the sick and by the hungry crowds, putting His arms around

The Created Person and the Mystery of God

the children—"let the little ones come to me," feeling the weariness of His disciples—"come away by yourselves and rest awhile."[156]

(3) JESUS HAS A SINGULARLY PROFOUND CAPACITY FOR HUMAN RELATIONSHIPS. Jesus desires to live with people, with *particular* people. The disciples who gather around him are not a philosophical school; they are a group of friends who share the whole of life together. Jesus calls each of them by name, and he knows their personalities, their fears, their strengths and weaknesses (Nathanial he calls "guileless," Peter is the Rock, James and John the Sons of Thunder). He opens up to them the truth about life with great gentleness and with a concern that each will embrace it personally. And in his great agony he longs for his friends to stay and watch with him; their tiredness and incomprehension cause him sorrow, as does the subsequent betrayal of Peter. But his desire to remain with them is greater than all their weakness. "I will not leave you orphaned. I will come back to you. I go to prepare a place for you, so that where I am you also shall be."

(4) JESUS HAS A DEEPLY DEVELOPED PERCEPTION OF THE VALUE OF LIFE AND TRAGEDY OF SIN AND DEATH. He weeps at the tomb of Lazarus, his friend. Jesus does not attempt to explain away death. He knows its evil, even as he takes its entire wrath upon himself. "Father if you are willing, remove this cup from me." No one has ever hated death more than

---

156 Romano Guardini offers some keen reflections on how the love of Jesus penetrates his emotional life and his engagement of the world. See *Jesus Christus*, trans. Peter White (Chicago: Regnery, 1959), pp. 87-88. Hereafter cited as Guardini.

Jesus. No one has ever known so well what a tremendous and awesome thing it is to live.

What we see here you might call "ordinary" human attributes—characteristics of Jesus that He has in common (at least in kind) with other good men. And yet in Jesus we see them in a special and exemplary way—we can glimpse an "ordinary humanity" that is really extraordinary, and that has been the model ever since for a *good man* (even today, few people would claim to be opposed to "imitating Jesus").

(5) The most powerful of these human attributes, however, is one that I would say is really peculiar to Jesus Himself in all of human history, at least with regard to the outstanding way that it forms all of His interaction with people, namely JESUS'S ATTENTION TO THE TRUTH OF THE HUMAN PERSON, AND TO THE "PARTICULAR PERSONS" HE MEETS. Indeed, what strikes us most profoundly about Jesus is the way He "looks" at human beings, the quality and intensity of His attention to the particular man and the particular woman. In fact, it is in the look of Jesus that humanity first experiences the meaning of the word "person". It is as though Jesus, with the whole force of His incredibly compelling and attractive character, says in front of every man and woman He meets, "You are a person." Jesus is entirely absorbed in a passion for the dignity and the destiny of the single person. No one in history ever looked at human beings in this way before; no one ever grappled with the individual person with such attention and insight and particular care. Even when He speaks to great crowds, Jesus' words are aimed at the heart of each person; they address the destiny of each singular person as though he or she alone matters. And those who "believe in Him," those who allow

The Created Person and the Mystery of God

themselves to be looked upon in this way, to be penetrated by this gaze, discover the mystery of their own personhood, the uniqueness and value of their own human faces. Those specific, irreplaceable persons whose figures were singled out by the look of Jesus shine brightly and unforgettably in the pages of the gospels. There is Levi the tax collector, immersed in his extortion: Jesus sees him one day and calls him; He is not scandalized by Levi's lies and thievery, nor by the unpopularity of Levi's profession. Jesus sees Levi the person, and He calls him. And as Levi "follows" Jesus, his true personality emerges and matures. He becomes one of the "Twelve"—one of those original witnesses whose testimony changes the world, and his personal experience of living day by day with Jesus is the source of what we know today as "the Gospel of Matthew". Then there is the woman who anoints Jesus's feet. The Pharisees see only a "sinner," a thing that they define entirely according to their own categories. Jesus sees a person. And in the amazing compassion with which He looks upon her, Mary Magdalen recognizes for the first time who she is, and that it is possible for her to live in the truth of her own dignity. "Woman, your sins are forgiven. Go in peace." Then there is that notable little man, Zaccheus, another criminal, who climbs a tree to catch a glimpse of Jesus. Jesus sees Zaccheus the man, the man with a heart full of curiosity and desire. Embraced by that look, the falseness of Zaccheus's life is shaken—he discovers himself, his capacity to act, to construct something true: "I give half my goods to the poor."

We see something tremendous in Jesus' attitude toward the person. It is creative. It reveals the person to his or her self. This is evident in the distinctiveness and particularity

Jesus Christ Preached by the Church

of those persons who follow Him. Peter, James, John, Mary Magdalen, The Woman at the Well, the two disciples on the road to Emmaus, the leper who returns to thank Jesus for his cure, the man born blind. Each of them is individual, and valued as such. Each too brings a creative participation to the drama that the gospels present. Jesus' humanity generates history, it generates life, it frees persons and opens them up to the clarity of their own selves.[157]

Yet, it still remains for us to consider the most astonishing characteristics of this man Jesus. We can consider, under two categories, those qualities of Jesus's humanity that—not only by the degree in which He possesses them, but also *by their very nature*—are special signs of His "being from God". These are characteristics of Jesus's humanity that *no other man has ever possessed.*

(1) THIS MAN JESUS HAS A UNIQUE AWARENESS OF GOD, AN INTIMACY WITH GOD, A SENSE OF GOD'S PRESENCE, A POSSESSION OF GOD'S AUTHORITY IN A WAY THAT HAS NO PARALLEL IN ANY OTHER FIGURE OF HISTORY. Jesus speaks about God and His relationship to God in a way that is totally unique. No other historical person has ever even come close to claiming such intimacy and even identity with the Creator of the universe. Indeed, great religious figures in history are usually distinguished precisely by the way they humble themselves in comparison to the ultimate Mystery of existence that they seek to

---

[157] This insight into Jesus's attention to the person is a central feature of the catechesis of Luigi Giussani. See for example, *The Origin of the Christian Claim*, trans. John Zucchi (Montreal & Kingston: McGill-Queen's University Press, 2000), ch. 8. Hereafter cited as *Origin*.

serve.[158] Jesus, however, lives and acts and offers Himself entirely out of the awareness that He (and He alone) "belongs" to God; He presents himself as being "on the same level" as the One whom he calls his *Father*.

(2) THIS MAN JESUS EXPRESSES HIS LOVE IN A "SUPERHUMAN" WAY. Jesus's way of loving surpasses every human measure—this is clear to us from what the gospels tell us about the intentions of His human heart. Above all we can see this in the way that Jesus accepts His own suffering and death. Jesus does not go to His death bitterly, nor even with stoic resignation. Jesus embraces His death. This act, this embrace of suffering, this allowing His flesh to be torn apart by the wickedness of people, *fulfills the heart of Jesus of Nazareth.* His humanity becomes an offering, available to every person.[159] Hours before the violence and rejection of the world that crucified Him—a violence into which you and I were born and in which we have shared—Jesus had already given the event of His death its definitive meaning, transforming it into a gift of His freedom and love, a gift of Himself: "Take and eat, this is my body, which will be given up for you...Take and drink, this is my blood, shed for you and for all in remission of sins."

This is truly amazing. It is clear that this particular man of history wanted Himself—His flesh and blood—to be the "food and drink" of every person on earth, to be the sustenance, the strength, the *life* of every person. What kind of love is this? It is the love of a man, but so different

---

[158] See *Origin*, ch. 3.
[159] Guardini speaks about the depth and the universality of the love of Jesus, pp. 89-97.

Jesus Christ Preached by the Church

from every human love, so different from every kind of love that we are able to muster up in our tiny hearts. All of our loves bump up against limits, but here is a limit-less human love. And it begins something new within history: "Do this in memory of me." It begins to change every human thing that it touches; it creates something new, a new people, a people drawn up into a limitless love, a people who—even with all of their weaknesses—begin to love in ways that their hearts have never loved before.

As we can see, Jesus is in every respect a man like no other man, a man whose humanity is so powerful that it defines forever the truth about being human. Jesus is the standard for man's imagination, for his conscience, for his aspirations. It is not surprising, then, that people today still want to salvage the image of this humanity from the wreckage of society's loss of supernatural faith. But the very figure of such a man is miraculous; it exceeds enormously every human capacity and energy. The only way to love Jesus's humanity, then, is to recognize THAT HE IS MORE THAN A MAN.

[2] God and Man in the Early Church

Any discussion of a Christian conception of the religious relationship between God and man will be greatly enriched by a consideration of those great Christian thinkers and writers of the first millennium known as "The Fathers of the Church." These men laid the foundations of a distinctively Christian world view by their vigorous engagement of the various religious, philosophical, historical and cultural issues of their times. By their teachings and writings as well as by the witness of their lives, these early Christian pioneers enabled the beauty and reasonableness of the truth about God and man to shine forth in the midst of the despair and disintegration of the civilization of late antiquity. Here we will take a look at several of the most important writers of the "Patristic" age, noting how they contributed to a proper religious understanding by responding to specific challenges both from the surrounding culture and within the Church herself. We will see how the Fathers provide the perennial model of the Christian *Apologia*: the reasoned defense of the Christian proposal against its attackers and distorters, and the manifestation of that proposal as the definitive "answer" that corresponds to the mystery of man's vocation and the need of the human heart for truth, goodness, and beauty, for a relationship with the Origin and Purpose of all things, for *happiness*. In fact it is, historically speaking, only in the context of Christian revelation and its explication that this fundamentally religious character of human existence (of which we have been treating throughout this text) becomes clear.

Jesus Christ Preached by the Church

The Fathers, by bearing witness to and unfolding the meaning of Divine revelation, also forged a genuinely Christian anthropology—a Christian understanding of man, his misery and his grandeur, his inescapable weakness and his indestructible hope. For all these reasons it is fitting, as we near the end of our reflections on the created person and the Mystery of God, that we offer a brief study of the patristic idea of God and man.

In order to appreciate fully what the Fathers accomplished in their times, it is worthwhile to examine briefly the classical world of late antiquity. At the time of Christ, the Roman Empire dominated the Mediterranean world from the Iberian peninsula through southern Europe and North Africa and on into Palestine and Asia Minor.

Rome had united many diverse peoples by means of its political and legal genius and its military and engineering skills. Traveling along all the roads of the Empire and benefitting from the *Pax Romana*, various cultural practices, philosophical speculations, and religious movements were brought into contact with one another and with the Greek humanism that formed the dominant intellectual tradition in the Mediterranean world.

On the surface, it might seem as though Christianity was simply one of many participants in a rich celebration of cultural diversity.[160] The truth, however, was that Christianity was the only "new" thing—the only truly living

---

[160] The Roman historian Tacitus (a.d. 55-117) had such a view of the Christian movement, although he expressed it in more pejorative terms. He saw it as one of many "mischievous superstitions" that could be found in first century Rome, "where all things hideous and shameful from every part of the world find their center and become popular" (*Annals*, XV:44).

force—in a civilization that had grown old and had begun to die.

Greek humanism, with its reverence for intelligence and for the disciplines of philosophy, art, poetry, and rhetoric, was hundreds of years removed from the sources of its original vitality. And the political and military success of Imperial Rome was haunted by great suspicions which—it seemed—only the exercise of force could lay to rest. Over a hundred years of wars and fierce political factionalism had made Romans deeply cynical about man's capacity for a rational and civilized life. The simple domestic and civic virtues that had formed the Roman character in previous centuries had been gradually replaced by a reliance on external power and intrigue and a lifestyle dominated by social status and material possessions.

Thus, it is not surprising that the world of late antiquity was morally decadent, and as we know from our own society, moral decadence breeds anxiety, dissensions, and violence as man becomes preoccupied with pursuing his ambitions and protecting his possessions. Then, in turn, the same decadence breeds dissatisfaction, boredom, and finally desperation as man begins to realize that his life is empty and without meaning.

Ancient Greco-Roman religion had nothing to offer as a cure for this complicated psychological and social pathology. The "official religion" of the Empire was still the old paganism, but it was an empty shell which did little more than serve the traditional Roman aristocracy's need for ceremony while adding a bit of color to the fringes of the popular imagination. Many educated and cultivated Romans paid their respects to the gods of the pantheon as a kind of ceremonial expression of a certain vague religious sensibility, one that contained a combination of noble intentions, lingering superstitions, and an overall fatalism in the face of what was perceived to be the ultimate cosmic force: *Fortuna*.

Others among the educated classes were not content with this, and sought higher truths through the practice of philosophy. The philosophical quest of late antiquity was carried out courageously and with great earnestness. And it cannot be denied that later pagan philosophers such as Epictetus and Plotinus—like their ancient predecessors—glimpsed profound truths about the nature of Divinity and the power of human intelligence and freedom. Nevertheless, both the Stoic and the Neoplatonic philosophies were vitiated from within by their own preoccupation with providing an escape from suffering and from the evils of the world. The Stoics, despite their respect for natural law and their intuition that Providence was universal and intelligent, could only succeed in rendering man's inevitable fate more bearable by investing it with rationality and necessity. Thus they considered the dissolution of man in death to be an inescapable feature of a divine order that was identified with the cosmos itself.[161] At the same time, the Stoics emphasized that man's present happiness and peace of mind consisted in a rational and volitional self-sufficiency that—among other things—tended to disdain compassion for the suffering of others.[162]

---

[161] For example, Marcus Aurelius says that one of the characteristics of the philosophic state is "waiting for death with a cheerful mind, as being nothing else than a dissolution of the elements of which every living being is compounded" (*Meditations* II:17).

[162] Thus Epictetus says, "the sorrow of another is another's sorrow, but my sorrow is my own" (*Discourses* III:10). This is not to say that the Stoics did

The Created Person and the Mystery of God

Neoplatonic philosophers, by contrast, spoke of the transcendence of the Divine Realm and of a transcendent destiny for the human spirit beyond physical death. St. Augustine would later remark that the Neoplatonists, in these respects, were closer to Christianity than anyone else in the pagan world. Nevertheless, for the Neoplatonists, man's transcendence was only accomplished by means of a radical separation from matter, including the material of his own body. The man who attains union with the Divine no longer has any relationship to the physical world and recognizes nothing therein as "good." Above all, his ego is freed from identification with corporeal existence; Plotinus said that the body surrounds the wise man like mere clothing—clothing, moreover, which he seeks ultimately to remove entirely.[163]

It is not hard to see why these difficult and ultimately life-denying philosophies appealed only to the intellectual

---

not believe in helping one's neighbor in time of need. Quite the contrary. Their understanding of generosity, however, was largely "utilitarian"—in that it limited itself to what could be done for another person in the external order of things—and above all dispassionate. The suffering of another was never to disturb one's tranquility; it was not to be shared affectively within one's own inner world. Stoic doctrine, therefore, went directly against the formal constituent of "com-passio." It is not surprising, therefore, that a man such as Marcus Aurelius—in spite of his noble and magnanimous nature—had no sense whatsoever of the meaning of Christianity.

163   See *First Ennead* IV.3-4. For the perfect man, the body is "mere clothing...not to be called part of him since it lies about him unsought, not his because not appropriated to himself by any act of the will." It is difficult to see anything less here than the dissolution of man's spiritual-corporeal unity. The famous observation made by Plotinus's chief disciple, Porphyry, is quite understandable in this context: he remarked that the master never spoke of his country of origin nor his parents because, apparently, he was "ashamed to be in the body."

elites. For the masses who sought meaning and purpose in their day-to-day life, there was a vast cafeteria of colorful and exciting new religions to choose from. Deities from Persia, Egypt and Syria made their way into the Roman world and became objects of devotion for a new style of religion known as the *mystery cult*. While a few of these cults espoused a high moral ideal, they did not propose a relationship with the divinity based on a proper notion of creaturehood. Rather the mystery cults sought to use techniques in order to appropriate divine power as a means of insuring survival and success against the implacable forces of death. In practice, the typical mystery cult combined obscure initiation rituals, magic, and sexual perversion with the promise of establishing intimacy with a particular god or goddess and securing his or her protection. The mystery cults generally provided neither a moral framework nor a higher perception of the divine. They were merely novel sources of distraction and superstitious illusion that enabled the common man to forget his own wretchedness for awhile.[164]

Side by side with the philosophers and the mystery cults and incorporating elements from both was that great decadent religious synthesis of late antiquity: Gnosticism. Gnosticism appealed to the human imagination by preserving the concreteness of religious rituals and practices, while at the same time it indulged human intellectual pride by promising to reveal to its initiates the

---

[164] Philip Hughes's *History of the Church*, first published in 1934, is still a perceptive study of the intellectual history of Christianity. Regarding the mystery cults, Hughes remarks that they were "a mixture of charlatanry and sensuality" that appealed to "the weakest parts of human nature" (*History*, vol. I, revised edition 1948 [London: Sheed & Ward, 1979], p. 70).

The Created Person and the Mystery of God

"higher knowledge" which is the secret meaning behind all religious symbols and practices. Gnosticism was already a powerful movement in the pagan religious world, but with the emergence of Christianity it became the first great enemy of orthodox doctrine as it quickly reinterpreted the events of Christ's life, death, and resurrection in gnostic terms.

In front of all this, the great concern of the Roman Emperors was to keep civil peace and maintain obedience to Imperial rule. This was the eminently practical justification for pagan Rome's religious policy, which involved both toleration of diverse religions and the establishment of a universal cult of ceremonial religious devotion to the Emperor and the State. The Imperial power wanted to ensure that every religious group would ultimately be subservient to the Empire, and it therefore sought to manipulate religious devotion for political interests. This attempt to subordinate religion to politics, however, was radically antithetical to Christianity—which took seriously the gesture of religious worship and the reality of its object. Hence the constant threat and frequent carrying out of persecutions against Christians who refused to worship the Emperor. The age of the martyrs only came to an end with the conversion of the Emperor Constantine and the promulgation of the Edict of Milan granting legal toleration to Christianity in 313.

It is important to stress, however, that the intellectual and social attitudes we have sketched here continued to be prominent forces in the world of the Fathers even after Constantine began the trend toward the "Christianization" of the Empire. The values and vices of late antiquity formed the mindset that would produce the great Christian

Jesus Christ Preached by the Church

heresies of the fourth and fifth centuries. After Christianity became the "civil religion" of the Empire, it gained many nominal adherents who remained at heart just as worldly, cynical, politically calculating, and intellectually proud as their pagan forefathers. Among these, heresy always found fertile ground. Moreover, the "Christian Emperors"—above all in the East—were still tempted to subordinate religion to political expediency; now, however, instead of persecuting Christians as a whole, they attempted to manipulate the internal affairs of the Church and often persecuted those who tried to defend orthodoxy or the freedom of the Church against imperial policies.

Thus we must say that the world of the Fathers was a world grown old, tired, and frustrated; a world in which the perennial human questions had taken on a seemingly unbearable weight. It was a world that had seen the spectacle of centuries of unavoidable human suffering, the inability of man to find fulfillment in any of his possessions or even in any of his ideas, and the failure of the highest forces of human ingenuity and civilization to secure a peaceful, harmonious life for the multitude of men. The inhabitants of this world sought an escape—by plunging into the irrational frenzies of animal sensuality or by soaring to the heights of a disembodied spiritualism where they would be protected from the pains of life.

In the very midst of this world, however, there came a new proposal, a possibility that the whole of life could be saved, that man—soul and body—could be saved; that man's weakness could be healed and his suffering invested with a magnificent dignity and beauty; that the impenetrable divine realm might open itself up and reveal itself to man—indeed *visit* man in his weakness and *help him*. This was

Christianity's invitation to the ancient world, which was based not on a new philosophical or religious system, but on an *event*—the event of God becoming man. This event was at the center of the witness given by the Fathers of the Church; and by their fidelity to it they transformed man's understanding of himself and the purpose of his existence.

The great labor of the Fathers of the Church was to testify to the mystery of Jesus Christ. They did not set as their aim the construction of a Christian world view, or a Christian philosophy, or a Christian culture and civilization. Nevertheless they laid the foundations for all of these, which developed as a consequence of the thoroughness and intelligence of their adherence to Christ. This adherence was enacted in a great variety of circumstances, and a good way to gain an appreciation for the patristic achievement as a whole is to focus on some key figures whose lives and work are able to furnish illustrative examples.

Let us begin with two great second century figures—one a "professional" philosopher and the other a bishop. The former, St. Justin Martyr, stressed that Christianity was the fulfillment of everything that was true and good in pagan thought; while the latter, St. Irenaeus of Lyons, passionately defended the uniqueness of Catholic truth against its Gnostic distorters.

Justin was born about the year 100 a.d. As a young man he became a seeker after wisdom, a philosopher, and he traveled from his native Palestine to Ephesus where he studied under both the Stoics and the Platonists. Fascinated by the Stoic doctrine of the immanent and pervasive presence of the Divine logos giving rationality to the whole cosmos, and also by the Platonist understanding of the natural kinship between the soul and the Transcendent

Jesus Christ Preached by the Church

Good, Justin was nevertheless dissatisfied by the incompleteness of the philosophic quest. He was also amazed by the remarkable courage and joy of the Christian martyrs he had seen dying for Christ while he was still a pagan. This admiration, along with the guidance of a Christian friend, led him to read the Scriptures. He soon discovered that Christ was the fullness of Wisdom, who had become incarnate in order to communicate the whole truth to man. He was the Goodness and Beauty sought by the Platonists, and the Divine Logos sought by the Stoics.[165] Justin converted to Christianity, but he continued to wear the "cloak" of a philosopher. He traveled to Rome where he opened a philosophical school that attracted numerous disciples. Finally, as his name indicates, he suffered martyrdom in Rome in the year 165.

Justin taught that Christianity was the fulfillment of philosophy and the correction of its errors. The philosophers had discovered portions of the truth, on account of the Divine Logos who enlightens the intellect of every man. But because they did not perceive the whole of the Logos—the whole of the Divine Wisdom—they contradicted one another and fell short of the full truth. Jesus Christ, however—said Justin—is the "Whole Logos" incarnate, manifesting in his flesh the fullness of the Divine Wisdom and making this Wisdom accessible not just to philosophers but to everyone. Thus, St. Justin concluded,

---

[165] Justin himself provides us with the information about his intellectual conversion in various places in the *Apologies*. See for example *II Apology*, ch. 12.

The Created Person and the Mystery of God

Christian revelation is "more noble than all human teaching."[166] It alone is the complete truth.

Justin the Christian philosopher also emphasized something that no philosopher had ever stressed before him—the meaning of history. Since the fullness of Divine Truth had become incarnate as a man in history, Justin concluded that the whole of human history had been a preparation for Him. This was clear enough in the case of the Jews; one could demonstrate that their prophecies were fulfilled in Christ. However, Justin was equally certain that philosophy had been given by God to the Greeks in order to prepare them for the Gospel. Justin saw the Incarnation as the center of God's plan for all of history, a plan that was destined to be fulfilled in the resurrection of the body and the renewal of all creation.[167]

In presenting Christianity as the fulfillment of the philosophic quest of the Greeks, St. Justin Martyr did not invent new speculations of his own, but sought to convey faithfully what God had really accomplished in history. We should not be surprised, therefore, that even in the middle of the second century St. Justin would place great emphasis on

---

[166] *II Apology*, ch. 10. "Whatever has been spoken aright by any men belongs to us Christians, for we worship and love, next to God, the Logos which is from the unbegotten and ineffable God...For all those writers were able, through the seed of the Logos implanted in them, to see reality darkly. For it is one thing to have the seed of a thing and to imitate it up to one's capacity; far different is the thing itself, shared and imitated in virtue of its own grace" (*II Apology*, ch. 13). Translations of patristic texts in this section are generally taken from the English edition of the *Enchiridion Patristicorum* made by William A. Jurgens. See Jurgens, *The Faith of the Early Fathers*, 3 vols. (Collegeville, MN: Liturgical Press, 1979).

[167] see *I Apology*, chs 5, 10, 18, 30ff, 46, 63; *II Apology*, ch. 6; *Dialogue With Trypho*, chs 95, 100.

tradition. Because Christianity is an adherence to a man in history—to the things he said and did and to the society he constituted—it was crucial from the very beginning to receive and preserve the authentic testimony of those He sent forth to bear witness to His name. Thus the measure of genuine Christian thinking and the anecdote to every poisonous distortion of the Christian message could only be fidelity to the apostolic tradition.[168]

It was also this fidelity that both guided and rendered fruitful the great work of St. Irenaeus at the end of the second century. Irenaeus was born in Asia Minor around 140 a.d. He travelled to Rome and to Southern Gaul and eventually became bishop in the city of Lyons. In Rome he first encountered the strange phenomenon of Christian Gnosticism, and he battled against it throughout most of his episcopal ministry in Lyons. Many Christians in Rome in the middle of the second century had become captivated by the theories of a charismatic preacher named Valentinus. After an unsuccessful attempt to get himself elected pope in 140, Valentinus broke openly from the Church and began to develop his own Christian gnostic sect. The general tendencies of the gnostic movement—its stress on esoteric and secret wisdom, its radical dualism between spirit and matter, and its hierarchy of divinities—resulted in a very peculiar interpretation of biblical revelation and the life of Jesus Christ. For Valentinus and his disciples, the God of the Old Testament is not the Ultimate Divine being, but an inferior and rebellious deity who created the material world

---

[168] In his famous account of early Christian liturgical and sacramental practice, Justin indicates that it was already common practice in the middle of the second century for the "memoirs of the Apostles" to be read at the Eucharistic celebration. See *I Apology*, ch. 67.

for his own evil purposes. Another more powerful deity called "Christ" was sent from the pleroma (the "society" of divine beings) to teach the truth and offer deliverance to lesser spirits who were trapped in this material prison. He inhabited the man Jesus—he certainly did not become incarnate—and by this means he taught secret doctrines to his initiates (the apostles). Needless to say, the Christ-deity (being no fool) abandoned the man Jesus before the messiness of the Passion got started.[169]

Behind the crassness and silliness of this highly imaginative distortion of Christianity we can recognize a perennial heretical principle: the denial of the historical drama of the redemption in favor of some purely theoretical or interpretive scheme that supposedly reveals to us the "real" significance of Christ and Christianity.

Irenaeus wrote his masterpiece—his treatise *Against the Heresies*—to combat Valentinianism and other gnosticisms that made their way up the Italian peninsula into Gaul. Throughout this great work, he contrasts the "secret knowledge" of the gnostics with the tradition handed down from the Apostles and preserved in the Church. Irenaeus stresses the consistency and reliability of this tradition, linked as it is to the real Jesus Christ of history. At the

---

[169] Our best source for the theories of Valentinus is books I and II of Irenaeus's *Against the Heresies*. Since the 18th century a number of original gnostic texts have been discovered, most significantly the "library" discovered at Nag-Hammadi in 1946. A reading of only a few of these texts is sufficient to convince us that Irenaeus gave an accurate report of the basic characteristics of gnostic thinking, and is therefore presumably a reasonably reliable source for the thought of Valentinus. For more on Irenaeus and Valentinus, and for an analysis of the Valentinian system, see R. A. Markus, "Pleroma and Fulfillment: The Significance of History in St. Irenaeus's Opposition to Gnosticism," *Vigiliae Christianae* 8 (1954), pp. 193-211.

same time he meditates more deeply on the unity of the Divine plan and the centrality of Christ's redeeming action. It is one God who creates all things visible and invisible and who recreates them in Christ. The world that is created through the agency of the Divine Word is *recapitulated*—brought again under the headship—of the Word made flesh, who, by coming into the world, embraces history and consecrates it to God.[170] Thus Irenaeus gave eloquent testimony to a theme that was original to Christianity: the unity and purpose of history centered on the Incarnate Word.

As the third century dawned Christianity passed through a brief period of toleration under the Severian Emperors. Indeed Alexander Severus (Emperor from 222-235) was a religious syncretist of apparently good intentions, who briefly legalized Christianity and even contemplated building a temple to Christ alongside the other temples he had for the other gods who engaged his eclectic interests.[171] It was during this period that a remarkable institution flourished in one of the great intellectual and cultural centers of the Empire: Alexandria in Egypt, which, among other things, had the greatest library in the ancient world. At the end of the second century, educated Christians under the sponsorship of the bishop established a "catechetical school" in Alexandria, which attempted not only to provide

---

[170] "Thus he sums up all things in himself, that as the Word of God is supreme in heavenly and spiritual and invisible matters, he may also have the dominion in things visible and material; and that by taking to himself the pre-eminence and constituting himself head of the Church, he may draw all things in due course unto himself" (*Against the Heresies* III:16.6).

[171] Hughes gives a good account of the religious interests of the Severian Emperors, *History*, vol. 1, pp. 162-164.

(for the first time) a systematic explanation of the Catholic faith, but also to explore its relationship with philosophy and culture. Its luminaries were the erudite and educated pagan convert, Clement, and his most famous disciple, Origen. This was a bold first attempt to carry out Justin's project in a scientific manner, to thoroughly explore the harmony between faith and reason, theology and philosophy. However, it was a deeply flawed effort.

Origen was a great genius with an unfailing personal devotion to the Catholic Church and the apostolic tradition, which he always carefully distinguished from his own private speculations.[172] During the persecution of the Emperor Decius he courageously confessed the faith, enduring imprisonment and torture that led to his death in the year 254. He wrote well over 1000 works, commented on the whole Bible, and engaged in polemics with Celsus, a formidable pagan critic of Christianity.

However, Origen's great intellectual project—an attempt at a synthesis of biblical revelation and Neoplatonic philosophy—did not succeed, and involved him in the unintentionally heretical speculations for which he is most famous today.[173] Nevertheless, Origen's influence on the

---

[172] "The teaching of the Church has indeed been handed down through an order of succession from the Apostles, and remains in the Churches even to the present time. That alone is to be believed as the truth which is in no way at variance with ecclesiastical and apostolic tradition" (*Peri Archon* I, preface, no. 2). Here Origen provides the orthodox criterion by which to judge his own theories.

[173] These include the following: the pre-existence of souls; the theory that the relation of soul to body was somehow the result of a "fall" (although Origen seemed to have held that the body was given to the fallen soul by God so that the soul could work out its salvation); the theory of apokatastasis—the ultimate reconciliation of all beings with the Divine

Greek speaking Fathers of the fourth century was enormous. In spite of his errors there was much that was profound in his theology. His emphasis on the co-eternity of the Son with the Father in the Trinity was crucial to the formation of St. Athanasius.[174] His biblical exegesis and his ascetical theology shaped the minds of the Cappadocian Fathers and inspired the young St. Jerome. And his personal devotion to the humanity of Christ and the redemptive value of Christ's sacrificial death tempered somewhat his Neoplatonic tendency to disdain the body.[175] Over a hundred years after Origen's death, St. Gregory Nazianzen would refer to this complex, flawed, but nevertheless pioneering Christian thinker as "the stone which sharpens all of us."

Principle, including the damned; the theory that the resurrected body will be something other than a human body—i.e. a "celestial" body of spherical shape. Many of these ideas can be found in the *Peri Archon*, an early work in which Origen attempts what he himself regards as very provisional speculations on matters regarding which he found no clear ecclesiastical teaching. It should be noted that the magisterial clarification of these points came long after Origen's death. He was no dissenting theologian.

[174] We find such in Rufinus's latin translation of the Peri Archon 4, 4, 1— here Origen refutes Arianism before its time by stating "there never was a time when He did not exist." It must be admitted, however, that Origen's trinitarian theology contains elements of subordinationism.

[175] This "personal devotion" is not always free from Platonic conceptualizations. Origen is at his best when dealing with the humanity of Christ as He exhibits Himself in the concrete soteriology of the gospels. For example, "the Lord when he took flesh was tempted by every temptation by which men are to be tempted. He was tempted for this purpose, that we might overcome through his victory" (*Homilies on Luke*, 29). Also: "When he took upon him the nature of human flesh he fully accepted all the characteristic properties of humanity, so that it should be realized that he had a body of flesh in reality and not in mere appearance" (*Commentary on Matthew*, 92).

The Created Person and the Mystery of God

From the middle of the third century until the Edict of Milan in 313, Christians endured two brutal and systematic persecutions under the Emperors Decius and Diocletian. Then, suddenly, the social position of the Church changed radically. The new Emperor was a convinced convert with a genuine devotion to the cause of the Faith. The contribution of Constantine the Great to the mission of the Church in the ancient world must be acknowledged. The peace he established for the Church in his domains allowed the Gospel to spread with a freedom hitherto unknown. The absence of violent persecution permitted the construction of new churches and (for the first time) monasteries where the life of faith could flourish without hindrance. At the same time, however, the Constantinian era introduced a host of new problems: now the battle lines were to be drawn more and more within the Church herself, and all too often the Christian Emperors were to favor the wrong side.

Less than five years after the peace of 313, the Church was plunged headlong into this new type of crisis. A popular, talented, and politically astute priest in Alexandria named Arius had developed a theory about the Trinity. Up until this time, most attempts by Christian thinkers to shed light on the unity and distinctness of the Father, Son, and Holy Spirit had been provisional at best. For Arius, classical Catholic accounts of the Trinity were dissatisfying and ambiguous and seemed to involve the Church in irrational and contradictory affirmations about God. He proposed a simple solution, logically coherent, easy to understand, and—at first glance—seemingly consistent with the language of the New Testament: God is one. He is the Unoriginate. The Logos, the Word, is his first and greatest creature. The Word is a reflection of the Divine Being, so

Jesus Christ Preached by the Church

perfect that he is called "Son" and God is his "Father" in a unique manner. Nevertheless, he is a creature. According to a famous slogan of Arius which he even set to music, "there was a time when he was not." This first creature fashioned everything else in turn; therefore he is called "god" in relation to the rest of creation; however he is not divine by nature. The Holy Spirit, too, is a creature, the first and greatest creature of the Word who is himself the divine-like creature of God the Father.

What Arius proposed was ingenious and remarkable. It appeared to be nothing less than a translation into Christian terms of the "Divine Triad" of Neoplatonism, in which Universal Intelligence and Universal Soul were inferior reflections emanating from the Transcendent One and bringing forth the spiritual and material world in turn. It seemed as though Arius had reconciled Catholic faith and philosophical wisdom, giving a rationally satisfying explanation of the Trinity.

In fact, however, Arius had *deconstructed the mystery* of the Trinity. His theory was condemned at the Council of Nicaea in 325, wherein the Only Son of the Father was proclaimed God from God, Light from Light, True God from True God, begotten not made, consubstantial with the Father. After this Council, however, the Arian party succeeded in gaining imperial favor by means of deception and intrigue. Enormous political pressure was brought to bear against orthodox bishops by Constantine's successors, and imperially sponsored synods tried to construct and then impose compromise Trinitarian formulations that secretly favored the Arian position.[176]

In the center of this storm was the singular figure of St. Athanasius, the great bishop of Alexandria and fearless defender of Trinitarian orthodoxy. Athanasius was exiled from his see no less than five times during his tumultuous career, because he stubbornly opposed any and every politically engineered compromise with the Arian position. Modern secular historians may often wonder why Athanasius was so passionate and so persistent about what might seem to be an abstract theological point. Yet we can appreciate the energy of his zeal if we realize that he perceived the deep connection between the mystery of the Trinity and the mystery of the Incarnation and Redemption. Athanasius's conviction about the Trinity was inseparable from his conviction about the Christian event and its significance for the life of man. Through the incarnation and redemption, God has made it possible for us to share in His very life. Our union with the Word made flesh gives us a participation in the Divine life. This is the great patristic teaching on *deification* ("theosis"): God became man so that men might become "gods"—that is, adopted sons of the Father. Athanasius perceived the radical implications of Arius's theories: if the one who became incarnate in the womb of the Virgin Mary was not fully Divine, how could he possibly give us a participation in the Divine life? In the Arian system, the magnificent destiny of the Christian man comes crashing to the ground. The one who walked the

---

[176] For an extremely thorough and riveting account of the historical and political drama of Arianism after Nicaea, see Warren H. Carroll, *The Building of Christendom* (Front Royal, Virginia: Christendom College Press, 1987), pp. 9-43.

Jesus Christ Preached by the Church

earth, who became our friend, who gave us his flesh to eat and his blood to drink, was merely another creature like us. God has not shown us His face nor invited us into his friendship. He remains a stranger to us. Thus Athanasius declares: "the Son of God became Son of Man, so that the sons of man, that is, of Adam, might become sons of God. The Word begotten of the Father from on high, inexpressibly, inexplicably, incomprehensibly and eternally, is He that is born in time here below, of the Virgin Mary, the Mother of God, so that those who are in the first place born here below might have a second birth from on high, that is, of God."[177]

Moreover, if the Holy Spirit is not fully God, how can he possibly transform us into the likeness of God? "If the Holy Spirit were a creature, there could be no communion of God with us through Him. On the contrary, we would be joined to a creature, and we would be foreign to the divine nature, as having nothing in common with it...If by participation in the Spirit we are made partakers in the divine nature...it cannot be doubted that His is the nature of God."[178]

Thus for Athanasius, the full co-eternal divinity of the Word and the Holy Spirit was not only a truth about the

---

[177] *On the Incarnation of the Word of God and Against the Arians*, 8. "The fact is, then, that the Word is not from things created, but is rather Himself their Creator. For this reason did He assume a body created and human: so that, having renewed it as its Creator, He might deify it in Himself, and thus might introduce all of us in that likeness into the kingdom of heaven. A man would not have been deified if joined to a creature...neither would a man have been brought into the Father's presence if He [the Son] had not been the Father's natural and true Word who had put on the body" (*Discourses Against the Arians* 2, 70).

[178] To Serapion, I, 24.

mystery of God; it was also a matter of life or death for man—it was a truth decisive for the human vocation. Only the Divine Word made flesh divinizes His brothers in the flesh. If Christ is anything less than God, then the gates of heaven are closed and man is still in exile from his eternal home. The comfortable rationalism of Arius, in the end, robbed Christianity of its very heart.

The First Council of Constantinople finally brought the Arian crisis to a resolution in 381. This ushered in a period that is often termed the "golden age" of Patristic literature. The late fourth and early fifth centuries witnessed the splendid theological, ascetical, and mystical works of the Cappadocian Fathers—St. Basil, St. Gregory Nazianzen, and St. Gregory of Nyssa—and the courageous and beautiful preaching of St. John Chrysostom (it is interesting to note, however, that Chrysostom was driven into exile and eventually to his death by Imperial meddling in Church affairs). Meanwhile, in a cave in Bethlehem, St. Jerome applied his fiery temperament and his prodigious learning to a systematic and critical translation of the Bible from original languages. But the figure who towers over this period, who perhaps did more than anyone in the ancient world to impress a Christian form on human thought, is St. Augustine.

Indeed, the whole drama of these times is profoundly illustrated by Augustine's own life. Augustine experienced personally the frustration and inadequacy of the pagan culture; he sought satisfaction and peace through sensuality, the gnosticism of the Manichean sect, and Platonic philosophy. Finally, however, he came to Christ and—after many hesitations—entrusted himself to Him. Such is the personal story that is related unforgettably in the great

Confessions. And in retrospect, we can recognize that Augustine's conversion brought about a transformation of his entire personality. Indeed, it is doubtful that anyone would have remembered Aurelius Augustinus the pagan rhetorician and eclectic philosopher. But St. Augustine the bishop and doctor of the Church penetrated and shaped the understanding of an entire civilization for over a thousand years, and still deeply affects the Christian mind today.

The combination of a gigantic and lucid intellect and an intense personal awareness of the mercy of Christ dominated Augustine's theology. His attachment to the Church and his conviction about Catholic doctrine were strengthened by the fact that he himself had tried so many false paths that led nowhere.

As a Christian convert, Augustine took up immediately the task of exposing the falseness and futility of his former Manicheanism. The Manicheans were the highly organized successors of the earlier gnostic movements. Their doctrine was a variation on the general features of gnostic mythology: the universe was radically dualistic, with spirit and matter (light and darkness) constituting antithetical principles. Man was a spark of the divine spirit trapped inside the darkness of matter. What attracted the young Augustine (and many others) to the Manicheans was that this dualism within man appeared to exonerate him from responsibility for the sins of the flesh. Since the body was an evil and constraining force opposed to spirit, certainly the spirit of man could not be held accountable for the nasty things the body did. At the same time, Manicheanism promised to initiate its devotees into a comprehensive wisdom that would explain all the secrets of the universe. Thus Manicheanism capitalized on the dominant cultural

The Created Person and the Mystery of God

trends: unbridled sensuality, speculative curiosity, and the desire to escape the burdens of life through intellectual enlightenment and religious technique. Augustine was an initially enthusiastic adherent of the Manichean sect, and he remained a member for nine years. In the end, however, he discovered that the entire system was an elaborate tapestry of illusions, frauds, and nonsense.[179]

In making the conversion from Manicheanism to orthodox Christianity, Augustine grasped two basic truths that shaped the whole of his intellectual vision: the mystery of creation and the freedom of the human will. St. Augustine enshrined forever in the Christian consciousness the deep conviction that the physical world is good. There is not opposition between the realm of the Divine and the material creation; rather, there is a vital subordination in which the created reality—shaped according to the Divine Wisdom as a reflection of God's own perfections—constitutes a *sign* pointing toward the One who fashions it and keeps it in being.[180] Man's experienced tension between soul and body, and between the spiritual and the material, is not the result of some ontological flaw inherent to matter;

---

[179] An extensive account of his own experience as a Manichean, as well as an exposition and refutation of the main Manichean tenets, can be found in Augustine's *Confessions*, books III, IV, and V.

[180] "Ask the world, the beauty of the heavens, the splendor and arrangement of the stars; the sun that suffices for the day; the moon, the comfort of the night; ask the earth, fruitful in herbs and trees, full of animals, adorned with men; ask the sea, filled with so many swimming creatures of every kind; ask the air, replete with so many flying creatures. Ask them all, and see if they do not, as if in a language of their own, answer you: 'God made us'" (*Sermon* 141:2). St. Augustine is certainly one of the key theologians in the whole history of religious thought to perceive and expound upon one of the central themes of our thesis: the creature as *sign*.

rather it is a consequence of the free misuse of the human will when it seeks to love creatures without regard to those creatures' intrinsic reference to the Creator. Thus Augustine's famous phrase, "it is not the bad body that causes the good soul to sin; it is the bad soul [through the bad use of its will] that causes the good body to sin." Augustine insists that "every good is from God. There is no nature, therefore, which is not from God. That movement, however, of turning away from God is what we acknowledge as sin, because it is a defective movement and every defect is from nothing. See whence it comes, and you may be certain that it does not come from God. Nevertheless, because it is voluntary, this very defect lies within our power."[181]

At the same time, Augustine's extensive and personal familiarity with the lure of sin and the restlessness of the human heart as well as the liberating and transforming power of God's love shaped his conviction about the absolute necessity of divine grace. Later in his life, when Pelagius tried to argue that the human will was self-sufficient, able to perform the good and bring man to his spiritual perfection by its own innate power, Augustine developed his great theology of grace. Man's free will has been wounded by original sin and is therefore alienated

---

[181] *On Free Choice* 2, 20, 54. Elsewhere Augustine indicates how an evil will involves grasping a thing outside of the context of its natural ordination to the Superior Good. "For the evil is not in the things which occasion our fall, but in the fall itself. The things which cause our fall are not in their own nature evil; but our fall is evil because *it is a reversal of the natural order, since it proceeds from the highest level to the lower*. Greed is not a fault belonging to money; it belongs to the man with a perverse love of money who abandons justice, which ought to be regarded as incomparably better than riches" (*City of God* 12:8, emphasis added).

from God and disoriented with regard to its true Good. By grace, God takes the initiative by inclining the will toward Himself, by placing within the heart of man an attraction, a fascination with Divine goodness and beauty that offers man freedom from the dissipations of inadequate goods. It is this grace of God—preceding any merits on the part of man—that empowers the will to turn away from its attachment to sins and move freely toward God. Even though God's grace takes the initiative, strengthens the action of the will from within, and brings it to perfection, nevertheless the will must freely co-operate with God's action. "We too work," Augustine concludes, "but as fellow-workers with Him who does the work, because His mercy anticipates us."[182]

Such was the Augustinian conception of grace that became a fundamental feature of the Christian understanding of man. Although Augustine, in forging his theory, fell into an excessive and inaccurate view of "predestination," still his fundamental insight into the synergy of divine grace and human freedom distinguished the basis for Christian moral activity and gave to the Christian man a hope for the attainment of virtue and goodness that none of his pagan predecessors ever had.

When St. Augustine finally died in the year 430, the collapse of the Western Roman Empire was under way, as

---

[182] *Nature and Grace* 31:35. See also *Grace and Free Choice* 17:33, and *Homilies on John* 26:2-7. In another text which is representative of Augustine's conviction that grace is an interior empowerment, he notes that "it is not by law and doctrine sounding from without, but by an internal, secret, wonderful and indescribable power that God works in men's hearts not only true revelations but even good dispositions of will" (*The Grace of Christ and Original Sin*, Book I, 24, 25).

waves of barbarians poured into the Mediterranean world. Meanwhile the doctrine of the Church was in the throes of another crisis. Once again that central question arose: "Who is Jesus Christ?" The Arians had denied that Christ was truly God. In the beginning of the fifth century, Nestorius, the Patriarch of Constantinople, made a similar denial for a different and more subtle reason: he claimed that the man Jesus Christ was merely a human person mysteriously united to the Divine Person of the Word. After this heresy was condemned at the Council of Ephesus in 431, its opposite quickly developed—the heresy of monophysitism, which claimed that the Incarnate Word possessed only a Divine nature, that by taking flesh in the womb of Mary He somehow absorbed the humanity into His divinity.

These two challenges—the fall of Rome and the monophysite heresy—were met by the same man, a pope, one of only two popes in history who bears the name "the Great." St. Leo assumed the chair of Peter in 440. During this time of social collapse the people of Rome looked to Leo for temporal as well as spiritual leadership. Leo did not disappoint them. In the spring of 452, the ruthless Huns and their legendary leader Attila were camped outside the walls of Rome. They had pillaged their way through Eastern Europe, and no one had been able to withstand their vicious force. Leo, however, went forth into the invader's camp and boldly demanded an audience with Attila himself. There is no record of that mysterious conversation. What we do know, however, is that Attila turned around afterward and took his unconquerable plundering army

The Created Person and the Mystery of God

away from the city and out of Italy entirely. Rome was spared from certain destruction.[183]

Leo, however, always knew that his primary task was the spiritual shepherding of Christ's flock. A magnificent collection of his sermons covering the whole of the liturgical year reveals to us the depth of his preaching.[184] Leo's greatest achievement, however, was his clear and authoritative articulation of the mystery of the Incarnation. In his famous letter to Flavian, bishop of Constantinople, he drew the lines of orthodox Christology which have remained firm to this day. The one Person of Christ, eternally begotten of the Father as to His Divinity, took a full human nature in the womb of Mary and became a man like us in all things but sin. The human nature and the Divine nature are united in the mystery of His Person, but they remain distinct and possessed of all their essential features: Christ's human nature is not absorbed, or merged, or comingled with the Divine nature so as to lose its proper character. This letter, known as the "Tome" of Leo, was read aloud to the bishops assembled at the Council of Chalcedon in Asia Minor in the year 451. The bishops, in their endorsement of the letter, proclaimed: "Peter speaks through Leo!"[185]

---

183 Carroll, p. 119.

184 These sermons make a significant contribution to the present Office of Readings in the Roman rite.

185 "While preserving, therefore, the quality proper to each nature and joining both in one Person, lowliness was taken on by majesty, weakness by strength, and mortality by eternity...In the whole and perfect nature of true man, therefore, the true God was born, complete in what pertains to His own nature and complete in what pertains to ours" (Letter 28, 3).

Leo's conviction that Christ is true man had as one of its key motivations the same concern as St. Athanasius a century ago: the redemption and divinization of men. Just as Athanasius saw clearly that Christ must be truly God if he is to give man a participation in the Divine life, so Leo perceived that—in order to really save and recreate our humanity from within—Christ had to be fully *one of us*. Leo understood that the redemption was not an abstract decision by God to ignore our sins but an event in history in which man is really changed, human nature is really made new, sin and death are really overcome. If Christ did not fully possess our nature, then he did not redeem our nature, he did not bring our humanity back into the presence of the Father. "By what means could He fulfill the true role of a Mediator, if He that was, in the form of God, equal to the Father, were not a sharer also of our nature, in the form of a slave, so that through the new Man there might take place a renewal of the old, and the bond of death contracted by the wrong-doing of one man might be loosed by the death of one Man, who alone owed no debt to death?"[186] This explains both the urgency and the clarity of Leo's insistence on the true humanity of Christ.

In conclusion, let us recall how the Fathers of the Church—by testifying to Christ and the Church and devoting their intelligence to the defense and deeper understanding of the Faith—introduced into the world a new understanding of man, the purpose of his life, and the means to attain happiness. The ancient pagan culture, frustrated by the apparent aimlessness of temporal life and

---

[186] Letter 124, 3.

the inaccessibility of the divine, took refuge in fatalism or gnostic fantasies. The preaching of the Fathers, however, introduced an entirely new idea that has become the basis of the Christian view of the world: the idea that history is governed by Divine Providence toward a precise goal, that this goal has been revealed at the center of history, and that it is nothing less than the revelation and communication of God's wisdom and love to the world. Moreover, the pagan world—unable to overcome sin and all the divisions it introduced into the life of man—succumbed to the temptation to define sin and evil as necessary constituents of a cosmic process which must somehow be escaped. The body and the material world were viewed by many as necessarily evil, since they were the most removed from the simplicity of the divine and the most apt to distract man from the nobility of his own nature. Against this tendency, manifest in pagan thought and Christian heresy alike, the preaching of the Fathers emphasized the goodness of the physical world, its positive purpose of reflecting God's goodness and pointing man toward Him, and its share in the dignity of man's vocation in Christ who has assumed flesh and risen in the flesh. Moreover, the cause of disunity in the universe and in the life of man is not a battle between divinities or a dualism of spirit and matter; it is man himself who does not *direct his free will* in accordance with the exquisite harmony and purposefulness of all things established by God. And in response to the pagan frustration over the wretchedness of the human will, the Fathers preached redemption: the power of God's grace and the tenderness of His mercy. Man, in spite of all his sins, is destined to be transformed and recreated, to become "godlike"—not by his own power, but by the power of God

Himself and by the magnificent condescension in which God came to heal man by becoming man, to raise us up to Divine life by bringing the fullness of that life into our midst. The Trinitarian and Christological heresies of the fourth and fifth centuries would have separated man from God and would have left him, in the end, no better off than the philosophers of late antiquity who gazed up at heaven with erudite despair or the gnostics who spun webs of fantasy about a Divinity who remained remote and inaccessible above the layers of the heavens. In the final analysis, the Christian *apologia* of the Fathers is nothing more than their reasoned witness to Christ Himself, God and man, the Way, the Truth, and the Life.

[3] A Note on the Church

We will conclude our reflections on man's relationship to God by bringing that relationship to its most concrete level for the particular person in this present moment. Analysis of man's religious nature, metaphysical speculation, and the teaching of Christianity ultimately still leave me with the concrete question: "where do *I* find the answer to *my* life?" Everything we have spoken about, in fact, does have an immediate, accessible reference point available to each of us here and now. Thus, it is fitting that we conclude with a word on the "Church".

The concrete reality of the Catholic Church as the continuation of the presence and action of Jesus in the world is a particularly crucial point to which we must bear witness in the world today. In the midst of a culture of loneliness and absence of meaning, people have begun to rediscover the beautiful and compelling life of Jesus of Nazareth and the claim he made about himself and the relationship of every man to himself. "I am the Way, the Truth, and the Life. No one comes to the Father except through me." More and more people experience the exhilarating conviction that this Jesus of Nazareth possesses the key to the mystery of human existence and that they must therefore follow him without reservation. There is a great desire among those who rediscover Jesus to entrust themselves to him completely, to "do whatever he tells you." This desire, however, gives rise to a puzzling and often agonizing question for the person of today—"How do I follow him?"

Jesus Christ Preached by the Church

In Palestine in 30 A.D. the answer to this question had a certain direct circumstantial simplicity to it. One could go up to the Master and simply say, "I want to be your disciple." The original disciples followed Jesus by actually, physically following him around, listening to him, doing what he asked them to do, spending time with him and watching him, making him the model of their lives, receiving his healing power, his grace, his forgiveness. Then, Jesus ascended into heaven; his humanity took its definitive place at the center of all creation from which he would rule as Lord of all the universe and Lord of all history.

So now he's in heaven. But I'm still on earth. How do I follow him now? If I were living in the time immediately after the Ascension, the question would still have been relatively uncomplicated from a sociological point of view. There were these 12 men who had spent a lot of time with him, who knew him intimately—I would go stay with them, watch them, do what they told me to do. In fact, Jesus pointed these men out explicitly: he said to them, "He who hears you, hears me." They were the men that Jesus has directly "sent" to continue his work. If I spoke Greek I would refer to this "sending" by calling them "apostles." The apostles are the emissaries of Jesus; they are the direct "link" with the humanity of Jesus.

But now two thousand years separate us from Jesus and his apostles. How can I be in vital contact with Jesus now? If Jesus says, "no one comes to the Father except through me...no one attains to the goal and the fulfillment of his existence except through me"; if he means that I am obligated to believe in him and follow him now, in the 21st century, then he must have established some means whereby I can be in contact with him. What does it mean to belong to Christ today? When I look around, I see a lot of people who call themselves Christians, "followers of Christ" (which is what I want to be). And yet everybody says different things. There are all these different, competing claims about "the true way to follow Christ." How do I judge between them? How can I determine which way is the true way? Remember, if Jesus really made the claim to be the salvation of men in all times, then there must be some concrete possibility to follow him now.

One thing that is clear from the Gospels is that Jesus gathered a community around Him. Indeed, He *founded* a community, specifically selecting disciples to live in communion with Him; disciples who in turn would enlarge this community after His Ascension. Why did Jesus found a community?

The general background to Jesus's *explicit* intention in founding the community of His followers as a historical and social entity is based on *the implications of the Incarnation itself.*

We know the dogma of the Incarnation, we know the history of how it was clarified in general councils and explicated by the great Fathers of the Church. Jesus is true God and true man, consubstantial with the Father in His Divinity and united with us in His humanity according to every proper aspect of human nature (body and soul, senses, human intellect, human will, "human heart"—the Most Sacred Heart of Jesus is a human heart in every respect)—we say that He "became like us in all things but sin". We also know (and this is the only way that Christianity can even be taken seriously as a religious proposal) that the

Incarnation is a *real event* that took place. God the Son took on a human nature in the womb of a 14 year old Jewish girl named Miriam of Nazareth, He was born, He lived, He worked, He preached and healed, He gathered followers around Him, He suffered on the Cross, He rose from the dead—He, the Creator of the universe. The Incarnation has to do with events of history, with *particularity*, with a human concreteness that you can point to. The Incarnation is *not* an abstract "mythical" symbol that "didn't really happen" but that supposedly illustrates some universal, cosmic truth about "God's closeness to man". The fact that is abundantly clear to man's natural religious sense is the *distance* of God, the gulf between the Infinite and the finite that calls forth wonder, adoration, and love, but also *precludes* direct accessibility to God. Man is not interpersonally close to God according to nature. Only an event, springing from the Divine initiative, can establish that intimacy. Thus the Incarnation is not a myth or a philosophico-religious principle about some kind of essential Divine-human closeness or natural interpersonal unity. The Incarnation *is the historical event in which God draws close to man*. God is man's intimate companion, not for some necessary philosophical reason, but because God has decided to reveal Himself to man *by means of man*.

God's becoming man is the *method* through which He reveals Himself and communicates His grace to man. The Incarnation is the summit and the defining moment of God's method of dealing with man.

How can we summarize this "Divine methodology"? GOD USES MAN AS HIS INSTRUMENT. From the beginning, man's humanity is the means through which God intends to reveal and communicate Himself. This is true starting on page one of the book of Genesis: Adam, a single man, in intimate union with the single-hearted cooperation of his companion Eve, was given the spectacular responsibility of being "Head of the human race," of being the instrument through which the supernatural grace and vocation of each human being was to be *transmitted*; in the original plan of God, being a son of Adam should have brought with it divine grace as its proper inheritance. But as we know Adam and Eve *failed* in this singular task, and as a result the nature that we inherit from them *lacks* the very grace that God intended for it to have, without which it cannot achieve the supernatural purpose for which God created it. But God did not abandon the man He created. He began immediately to work for the restoration of man, promising that a son of Eve would redeem the human race. God's plan to restore the human race takes place through the mediation of human beings whom He chooses to be His instruments. We see this very precisely in the Old Testament, in what is often called "salvation history". God's plan passes very concretely through Seth and his descendants to Noah to his son Shem and his descendants down to Abraham, Isaac, Jacob, Joseph, and then Moses and the people of Israel—a defined group of human beings linked to a particular piece of land—with their kings and their temple and above all their great prophets, and finally one daughter of Israel, Mary, who becomes the perfect instrument of God and bears a Son whose humanity is not simply "used" by God but is united to the very Person of God the Son.

Here you can see the grand unity of sacred history—God constitutes a people as His chosen people, forms them by means of prophets through whom He communicates His

Jesus Christ Preached by the Church

truth to them, all in preparation for the climactic moment when He Himself will become one of those people. Thus the Invisible, Unapproachable God reveals the mystery of Himself through a visible, audible, tangible man. This is God's method—THE INVISIBLE, THE SPIRITUAL, THE SUPERNATURAL IS REVEALED AND GIVEN *BY MEANS OF* THE VISIBLE, THE MATERIALLY CONCRETE, THE HUMAN REALITY WHICH BECOMES THE "VEHICLE" OF SOMETHING INFINITELY BEYOND ITSELF. Indeed we can sum up this method—"the method of the Incarnation"—in one word: SACRAMENT.

And we must say, this method makes a lot of sense. Visible, material, human realities are the starting point of every man's knowing process—thus the "easiest" way for God to communicate with man is to make Himself available to man right here, in the world of visible, tangible, sensible realities where man's knowledge begins. This is an approach that is adapted to *all men*, not merely philosophers and mystics. It is also an approach that is wonderfully *merciful* to fallen man—we poor human beings who in our disorder are always seeking our fulfillment among the limited things of the world suddenly come upon Something in the world that really does correspond to our hearts. This is what the Incarnation is all about; as St. John expresses it in his first letter: "What we have *heard*, what we have *seen*, what we have looked upon and *our hands have touched*—THE WORD OF LIFE"!

God became man so that He could be seen, heard, and touched, so that He could teach with a human voice, so that He could stretch forth a human hand over a person and say "your sins are forgiven," and—in the ultimate humiliation

The Created Person and the Mystery of God

to which He was impelled in His gratuitous love—so that He could break His human body on the Cross and distribute it as "food and drink" to the whole human race, so that His death-defeating, immortal, risen human flesh could generate the resurrection of the flesh of all those who eat His body and drink His blood.

God became man so that He could be seen, heard, and touched...Now of course, there is always a sense in which Divine truth and the Mystery of God are *in*visible—indeed God is *invisible as such*, which means that He Himself can never become subject to the limitations of sense objects and the judgment of sense or even human intellectual knowledge.[187] After all if I merely *look* at Jesus my senses and my mind tell me "He's only a man". God does not *reduce Himself* to what is visible; He does not reduce His Mystery to the limitations of earthly realities. But He does communicate His Invisible Mystery *through* visible realities; which means that even though I don't see the invisible essence of God when I look at the humanity of Jesus, nevertheless my encounter with the humanity of Jesus *is the starting point for faith*; it is the *way* that my heart and soul come to know (by faith) who God is.

Jesus's living humanity is the method by which God wills to communicate His grace and revelation to man. This is the method that follows as a consequence of the Incarnation, and it is the method that is most adapted to the condition of man who walks through the world of space and time. THEREFORE, THIS SAME METHOD MUST

---

[187] We have examined extensively above, in Part II, the reasons why this is so.

CHARACTERIZE THE WAY THAT GOD SAVES ME TODAY. Why did Jesus rise from the dead? Was it to become *less* present, *less* active, *less* effective in His saving mission? Why did Jesus ascend into heaven—was it so that the revelation He brought might cease to present itself to our senses, might remove itself from human history, becoming once again intangible, unapproachable, distant? Was it because He didn't want to meet people one-on-one anymore, didn't want to call them personally, to accompany them personally in their lives, to forgive their sins *personally*?

On the contrary. In the Resurrection and Ascension, Jesus's humanity is transfigured and perfected; it does not cease to exist or cease to be significant. His humanity becomes greater, and the human energy of His mission becomes more extensive—after the resurrection Jesus becomes more capable (not less capable!) of being present on the roads of the world. Jesus's humanity has reached its perfection, and that means a perfection of His humanity's capacity to *mediate* salvation to man, to be humanly present in the concrete life of man.

Therefore, today, in the year 2003, I should be able to find a community of the followers of Jesus who *still have access to His humanity* in all of the human facets that He displayed during His earthly mission. The "place" in the world today where I can follow Jesus must be a place in which His mission continues to be carried out visibly, audibly, tangibly in all of the aspects that are proper to it. There must be a human reality in the world that continues the human presence of Jesus. "I am with you all days, even unto the consummation of the world."

If I were in Judea and Galilee in 30-33 a.d. I would have been able to interact immediately with Jesus. I could have listened to His teaching with the certitude that it was God's teaching, and the certitude that it had not been corrupted since it was coming directly from the mouth of God's definitive instrument. I could have listened with confidence that this one human voice was to be followed over all the other conflicting voices including the confused voice of my own narrow subjectivity. I could have obeyed the will of this man, done the things He told me to do, practiced His demands in my life, confident that His will was the expression of the will of God for my life. I could have gone up to this man and told Him all my sins, and when He said "your sins are forgiven" I would have known that God had forgiven my sins in that very moment when Jesus enunciated these words with His human voice. I could have stood at the foot of the Cross in the very moment when He was dying for my sins; I could have touched His Risen flesh with my hands, and sat with Him at table when He broke bread and said, "take this and eat, this is my body."

These are the human gestures and human actions through which Jesus saved people. Therefore, even today, I want to be in touch with these saving human gestures and human actions of the God-man.

Thus the place where I can follow Jesus today must be the place where His teaching continues with a single voice, His instruction continues through a single authority, and His sanctifying work continues through human gestures that communicate Divine life. Unless all of these aspects are available to me now, how can the *humanity* of Christ be my salvation?

Jesus Christ Preached by the Church

Is it enough to have a book that tells me about what He did 2000 years ago, with some merely interior assurance that it applies to me now? It is enough for me to have a book—even a book that I believe to be Divinely inspired—is it enough for me to have a book about a man who did things 2000 years ago, things the human images of which I have to reconstruct with my own imagination? Is it enough to have maybe a group of people with whom I can talk about Jesus and try to stimulate my memory and emotions with words spoken about His *absent* humanity? Is it enough to have God as a "spiritual presence within," as though after the Incarnation, Death, and Resurrection of Jesus, God suddenly decided to abandon the method of using human realities as His instruments, and instead to give direct, interior, spiritual subjective revelations?—revelations, moreover, about which everyone disagrees and which each interprets in his own way, so that the clear human voice of Jesus can no longer be distinguished in the cacophony of conflicting testimonies to inner experiences?

Or is there a hypothesis which is much simpler, more consistent, more adequate, more in keeping with the kind of man Jesus was and the character and intent of His mission? The very nature of Jesus's presence in the world as God Incarnate suggests that the fundamental characteristics of this presence must continue if Jesus's saving work is to continue. This means that, in *some* humanly real way, the same possibilities for interacting with Jesus must exist today that existed in 30 a.d. Indeed the possibility of "encountering" Jesus must be *greater* now, not less! "Greater works than these you shall perform, because I go to the Father." Jesus rose from the dead and sent the Holy Spirit. Some Christians misunderstand the significance of

The Created Person and the Mystery of God

this, however. They believe that the Holy Spirit *replaces* the humanity of Jesus; that the work of Christ's humanity is over and done, and that everything is now left to the interior, illuminating presence of the Spirit testifying in the heart of the person. But in the Catholic understanding Jesus sends the Holy Spirit in order to deepen and amplify the mediation of His humanity, *not to lessen it*. The Holy Spirit effects the interiorization of what Jesus gives me through His sacred humanity, but my personal encounter with Jesus retains its human concreteness—Jesus remains humanly objective, "in front of" me and not simply "within" me (although He is *also* within me). Jesus became incarnate precisely so that man would not be alone in his own subjectivity, so that there would be a humanly perceivable reality in front of man to which man could submit himself, upon which man could depend. Jesus became incarnate so as to mediate the way, the truth, and the life to man from a "position" that is outside of his own subjectivity, a "reference point" that is objective for every man, "present" for every man. "No one has ever seen God; it is the Only Son, ever at the Father's side, who has revealed Him" (John 1:18). The tendency (among Christians over the past five hundred years) to locate the *primary* reference point of Christianity in the inner illumination of the Spirit rather than in an objective human presence (a presence to which the Spirit bears witness) has led us inexorably into the trap of subjectivism—ultimately, there is no objective authority that can ever tell me that my inner experience or personal interpretation is wrong, and there is no objective contact with the human concreteness of the Mediator who saves me. But I want (and I *need*) this contact! I am not pure spirit. I am not pure consciousness. I am a man of soul and body, and God became man so as to address me wholly, soul and body. "The flesh profits nothing"—but the "flesh" (sarx) is *not* the bodily aspect of my person, but bodiliness emphasized exclusively and in itself, bodiliness "cut off" from the soul, bodiliness that is not integrated into my personal reality as a human being. Christ's words "are spirit and life," but that means that they are spiritual in a way that *informs* life, human life; they are spiritual in a way that communicates life also to the body, that saves the body from degenerating into dead flesh and restores it to its integral place within the human person. Human spirituality without the body is as bad (probably worse) as human carnality unruled by the soul. The human being needs the integration of both; which is why he needs the mediation of the Incarnate Word.

This understanding of the Incarnation has implications for our question about "how to follow Jesus today". In the world of the 21st century, I must look for a *human* voice that teaches the truth of Jesus with consistency, with unity, with infallibility. I must look for a *human* authority to which I can entrust myself, which I can follow with confidence because the demands of this authority communicate to me clearly and unambiguously the will of Christ which is for the ultimate good of my person. I must look for those *human* gestures through which Jesus Himself calls me to be His disciple, strengthens me and sends me off to bear witness to Him, looks upon me compassionately and forgives my sins. I must find a way to "stand at the foot of the Cross"—to be touched directly, physically by that once-and-for-all sacrificial act that happened so long ago but that happened with direct reference to me.

If I were to find the place where all of these factors were present, I would find the place where Jesus continues to be present and where the saving mission of His sacred humanity continues to operate with all of the human immediacy suggested by "Incarnation". Indeed, I would find that place, that human and divine reality, called the Catholic Church.

Thus the very "logic" of the Incarnation—the truth that Jesus is the One Mediator between God and man, that God communicates salvation through His sacred humanity—leads us to a virtual "outline" of the Catholic Church as she exists today.

What we have observed about the mission of Christ's humanity is often expressed in Catholic theology as His threefold office of Priest, Prophet, and King. This means that the task of Jesus is to sanctify (as priest), to teach (as prophet), and to rule (as king). We see, too, that Jesus "commissions" the apostles, He "sends" His apostles into all the world—"as the Father has sent me, so I send you." The implications of this "sending" are clear: the apostles receive *a participation in Christ's mission*, so that the presence and action of Jesus will remain a living reality in the world—indeed so that it will *extend* throughout the world.

Thus we recognize Christ's presence in the world today when we see the full continuation of His mission. In the Catholic Church alone can we recognize in its fullness this continuation of Christ's mission. In her sacramental life we see the continuation of Christ's *sanctifying* work, above all the perpetuation of the work He accomplished once and for all on the Cross. Thus Jesus Christ the High Priest lives and acts in the Church's sacramental life. In the Church's magisterium we see a humanly identifiable and authoritative body of *teaching* that preserves and develops with consistency the implications of that Divine teaching which Christ gave the world in His Prophetic ministry. Thus Jesus Christ the Prophet lives and acts in the Church's magisterium, whose single voice and unshakeable fidelity to Christ's truth is guaranteed by the special office of the successor of St. Peter. Finally, in the Church's public and "structural" reality, in her "law," her worship, her spiritual and moral guidance, her authoritative formation and direction of the lives of her members, Jesus continues to speak concretely to the particulars of our lives; He continues to lead us, to *rule* us. Thus Jesus Christ the King lives and acts through the judgment of the Church's ministers and through the wisdom of her saints which is discerned and fostered by the Church's "shepherds".

God's method of dealing with man—the Incarnation, God's "becoming man"—requires as its compliment a fully human social reality to carry on the work of this man, a society, a "man writ large" that continues to be the objective, visible, historical, verifiable, encounterable instrument of the Divine presence and salvific will. Thus, the Church of Christ must be *a social reality that perpetuates in itself all the relevant human features of Jesus's mission.* Anything less amounts to a "disincarnation" of sorts, a movement *away* from an objective, historically consistent, here-and-now-in-front-of-me *reference point* for Divine authority in my life; a movement away from the "method" of the Incarnation and toward a subjective, historically divergent, unverifiable personal consciousness that I cannot distinguish from myself by simple objective criteria, and that leads inexorably toward gnosticism, immanentism, and atheism (and as we have already noted in Part I, Feuerbach has done us the service of mapping out with admirable clarity the inescapable logic of this degeneration from subjectivism to atheism). Attempts to justify this subjective turn in the name of the "work of the Holy Spirit" neglect the fact that the Holy Spirit works within man's interiority in accordance with man's nature as a *subject oriented toward objective reality*; that is, He leads man OUTWARD toward Christ and the Father.

These reflections on the "logic" of the Incarnation as God's method for dealing with man establish the fittingness, the appropriateness, the theological consistency that characterizes the relationship between Jesus of Nazareth and the visible, sacramental Catholic Church.

Because it mediates to us the real, glorified humanity of Jesus, the Catholic Church enables us to have a total, personal, life-changing relationship with Jesus. This is what the mystery of the Incarnation really means, and this is the way that it can concretely apply to my life. In the end this means a very simple and wonderful thing: I can be humanly close to Jesus. And in Him, I am united with God, the Mystery that fills and transcends the whole universe of being, the One for whom my heart has been made.

Conclusion

We can summarize the reflections we have made throughout these many pages, and articulate the direction in which they lead, in the following points:

My basic "stance" as a human being in the world is characterized by *realism*—regardless of what philosophical ideology I may profess, when I wake up in the morning and go about the business of my day, I am engaged by the realities outside of myself, the real beings in the world that get my attention, inform my mind, attract my interest and become objects of my choice, and move my life in some mysterious direction.

If I pay attention to this reality in which I am immersed and the way that I—by nature—respond to it, I can discover that the beings in the world that interest and attract me "point" to something beyond themselves—they do not exist sufficient unto themselves but point to some ultimate transcendent Cause and Perfection. Thus I am led to the reasonable conclusion that God exists, that He is the Source of all things (including me), and that I can find meaning and fulfillment in my life only by "returning everything to Him"–living for Him, the Infinite Good. My experience of the limited beings of this world convinces me that none of them can satisfy me. I can "become all things" in my knowledge and go "beyond all things" in my desire––I have a mind and will that are greater than everything that surrounds me, but that seek an infinite Greatness.

The most profound thing that I can say about myself, therefore, is that I am a religious being. My soul has the "task" of seeking the will of God, the Infinite Spiritual

Conclusion

Good, and of loving and worshipping God. I have a mind of spectacular grandeur, that is capable of coming to know the highest truths and indeed can reason to the existence of God Himself. I have a will that can love Him and a heart that can be struck by the reflection of His beauty. God's design is what corresponds to me and promises me a happiness that can never be taken away.

In several different ways, we have approached this key truth: the religious character of human existence. I am made to know and love the Mystery of God. Indeed the historical experience of humanity energizes this fact into an expectation, a hope, that is even greater than anything that I can imagine. Yet here, all that we have proposed, all our analysis, our metaphysics, and our observance of concrete human experience leads us to a kind of impasse. Thus our entire study prods us to explore further into the truth about religion.

I am confronted with a problem. The transcendent God who creates me and all things and inscribes the truth of His plan for my being indelibly upon my soul still seems so distant and so *easily ignored*. My soul is disordered, and instead of "following creatures all the way to their Source" I am constantly being distracted by them. Because of the disorder of my soul *I need God to "come closer"*, to enter into the visible world that clamors for my attention every day, to enter this earthly history with His revelation and *help me to know who He is*. I am made for God but I am not able to reach Him and I don't know the way to reach Him. Thus the only thing I can *reasonably* do is look around and see if maybe *He* has established a way. Because of my immortal destiny and my human weakness in front of that destiny, a claim made in history that God has revealed

The Created Person and the Mystery of God

Himself deserves my attention. It would not be reasonable for me to ignore it. It would be stupid.

There is a claim made in history that God has established the definitive way for man to reach Him. It is associated with a man named Jesus of Nazareth. If I am true to the tension that characterizes my concrete existence—that is, both my religious orientation and my failure to live according to it—then I *must* at least be *interested* in this proposal right from the start, and put some effort into investigating it with an open mind and heart. Who is this man Jesus, what did He say and do, what claims did He make about Himself? The only honest way to find out is to consider the image that clearly emerges from the historical testimonies to this historical man. From the start we can say this about this man: WHAT A MAN INDEED! His teaching is sublime, His human figure mysteriously and splendidly attractive, He embodies all that is most noble and true and good and wise about the human condition, BUT THEN THERE IS SO MUCH MORE! "He who sees me sees the Father"; "Your sins are forgiven"; "Sell all you have, give to the poor, come and follow me"; "I and the Father are One". This great, magnanimous, magnificent man claims to be God Himself. And then there are the miracles—so unpretentious and yet so astonishing and inexplicable: HE CLAIMS TO BE GOD AND HE ACTS LIKE GOD. I don't understand *how* this claim can be true, but when He says, "come follow me" it MAKES SENSE to follow Him. If I cannot trust this man to speak the truth of God then I cannot trust anything!

Okay, but *where is He now*? How can I "follow" Him now? How can He be the "way"—not only for people 2000 years ago—but also *for me today*? Through the visible

Conclusion

community of real people that He established to perpetuate His presence in the world, to make sure that this indispensable divine help can come concretely, visibly, tangibly into my life just like it did for the first disciples. He singled out particular individuals and said to them: "continue doing throughout the world this task that I came for—teach the truth about God, lead men to their salvation, baptize them, feed them with my body and blood, forgive their sins—extend my mission, my human presence into all the world so that through you I can touch every man and lead them to my Father IN THE SAME WAY THAT I HAVE TOUCHED YOU. Yes, I am sending the Holy Spirit into the world, but the mission of the Holy Spirit is not formless, private, interior, merely subjective illumination; the mission of the Holy Spirit is to bear witness to my coming in the flesh, to lead you to embrace my Risen Humanity present in the Church. I am with you all days..."

Jesus of Nazareth did not found a loose fellowship of people who observed Him and then gathered later to reminisce about Him. He founded a historical community of real people who are united from generation to generation, within which He continues to dwell not only "spiritually" but also "sacramentally"—so that even though my eyes don't see His human flesh, the "logic" of the Incarnation perdures in the world: from the moment of Mary's consent until the end of time there will always be a "place" in the world, in my tangible, temporal, everyday world, WHERE GOD IS REALLY PRESENT IN HIS HUMANITY—to nourish me, heal me, and through His sacramental ministers to teach me and guide and correct me, so that everything He began to do on the shores of the Sea of Galilee continues

The Created Person and the Mystery of God

today and *reaches me* right where my weak, sinful, distracted humanity needs it! In the end, the concrete *religion* that I must embrace with my whole being is the Church of Jesus Christ.

One final note: those of you who are already Christians should be aware of the fact that the path by which these things are discovered often follows not the "logical" sequence outlined here, but rather a more existential sequence. In fact, the existential process of reasoning might seem to follow the *opposite* order from the logical process we have presented above. This is especially true today. The person of today—living in a totally secularized culture that generates *illusions* on a scale never before known in human history—hardly ever thinks about God, or the metaphysical grandeur and existential misery of his human personal existence, much less his eternal destiny and the means to arrive there. The ordinary people we meet today haven't reasoned these things out (they don't possess the categories for thinking in these terms); yet still THIS IS WHAT EACH OF THEM *IS*—a heart made for God, an ineradicably metaphysical being, and by God's freely chosen design a *positive need* for Infinite Love. For them, reflection on these things *begins when they meet you.* They see, first, that your life is going somewhere, that there is meaning in your life—yes, you can and do fail, but you belong to something that enables you to grapple with everything that comes along, especially suffering and the disappointments of life. Even when you fail, you seem to have someplace to "put" your failure. WHERE DOES YOUR PEACE, YOUR JOY, YOUR INTELLIGENCE ABOUT LIFE, YOUR COMPASSION COME FROM? Obviously not from your own inherent greatness (this is one

Conclusion

of the reasons why God continues to allow us to fail)—WHERE DOES IT COME FROM? This is what gets the attention of your contemporaries, this is why they ask questions, this is even probably why they mistreat you. But you get their attention...they want to have what you have in your life. Remember, there is no "maybe" about this—THEIR HEARTS HAVE BEEN CREATED TO WANT WHAT RULES YOUR LIFE. They cannot be "neutral" in front of you. If they don't want to be *reminded* of what they're made for, they will persecute you and hate you, or else ignore you, slight you, marginalize you. But the other possibility is that they will want to belong to what you belong to. You belong to that community of those who follow Jesus of Nazareth. But who is He? The gospels and the tradition of the Church tell us who He is, and He teaches us that we were created for God. Thus, the psychological process of conversion often goes not from God to Christ to the Church, but from *the concrete witness of your life* (a life that is different from anything they've ever seen, but a life that renders visible in some way the Mystery of Eternal Love for which they have been created), to the Church that makes you the way you are, to Christ the founder of the Church who is God the Creator of all. Thus your participation in the living miracle of the Church is often the first impact of truth on those around you.

And it is real evidence—it strikes reason at the very core of its objectivity and judgment. For reason reaches its fulfillment when it says "yes" to Love.

About the Author

John Janaro is Associate Professor and Chairman of the Department of Theology at Christendom College in Front Royal, Virginia.

Printed in the United States
1026100003B/209